The Battle of Wakefield

30 December 1460

Frontispiece: Edmund, Earl of Rutland, pleads for mercy on Wakefield Bridge; engraving by W.S. Stacey. (G. Wheeler)

The Battle of *Wakefield*

30 December 1460

P.A. HAIGH

SUTTON PUBLISHING LIMITED

First published in 1996 by
Sutton Publishing Limited · Phoenix Mill
Thrupp · Stroud · Gloucestershire · GL5 2BU

British Library Cataloguing in Publication Data
A catalogue record for this book is available from the British Library

ISBN 0 7509-1342-8

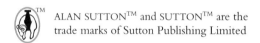

ALAN SUTTON™ and SUTTON™ are the
trade marks of Sutton Publishing Limited

Typeset in 11/12 pt Ehrhardt
Typesetting and origination by
Sutton Publishing Limited
Printed in Great Britain by
Butler & Tanner, Frome, Somerset.

Contents

For my mother

A Note from the Author

It was in May 1990 that I put pen to paper and began to write my first book dealing with the military aspects of the Wars of the Roses. At that time it was titled *The Forgotten Civil War*, which reflected my persisting belief that the military aspects of the Wars of the Roses are sadly lacking from the pages of other works on this period that contain the word 'Wars' in their title.

Five years later, that work was published under the title *The Military Campaigns of the Wars of the Roses*, and it was in effect the accumulation of many years research into the subject. Within that book I asked the following question: 'Have I achieved a factual written account of the battles of the Wars of the Roses?', and answered it with the following: 'My research has been long, my interest lifelong. I have done my best.'

Since then, I have often asked myself, did I do all that I could to ensure that all the relevant facts were contained within the book? I believe I did - considering the scale of the project, and the fact that it covered all fifteen battles fought in England between 1455 and 1487. However, there was one battle – Wakefield – which I felt warranted a more detailed study. Indeed, I am often amazed that one on this scale has not been done already. Perhaps the answer is that it is not generally held to have been a major engagement. While on this subject, let us consider the number of combatants present on the field of battle, which collectively could not have numbered more than thirty thousand. If we compare this figure against the possible eighty thousand plus present at Towton three months later, then by this standard, Wakefield was not a major engagement.

Likewise, if we consider the duration of the battle of Wakefield, which could not have lasted longer than two hours, and compare this against the mighty struggles at Barnet, Tewkesbury and Towton, then again, the answer seems to show that Wakefield was not a major engagement. However, putting scale aside, if we consider the consequences of the battle and its aftermath, and compare it to the other battles from the period in a similar manner, then no one can dismiss the battle of Wakefield as a mere skirmish. Indeed, Wakefield changed the course of English history.

It was Winston Churchill who wrote, 'Battles are the punctuation marks of history'; to which Jocelyn Stevens, Chairman of English Heritage, added his own version: 'Battlefields are the fragmentary pages on which those punctuation marks are written – in blood.' This comment was made at the national launch of the *Battlefields Register*, which is intended to help protect battlefields from destruction in this modern age – alas, its creation came too late for Wakefield, where much of the battlefield has already been 'developed'. However, it is still possible to trace the 'flow' of the battle from the vantage point afforded by the ruins of Sandal Castle.

It was in order to assist with this that I decided to write this book. Alfred Burne wrote his battlefield books in order to help 'Englishmen to find for themselves the actual site of the battlefields in their own neighbourhood, or on roads along which they may be travelling'. His words seem to fit this occasion more than adequately. I will, however, add the following, which is a quote from another fellow historian, Andrew Boardman, who wrote that battlefields are now 'the quiet places of history'. This is a statement that I often ponder when I walk the field of battle at Wakefield, especially early in the morning or late in the evening when the castle ruins and nearby park are devoid of the crowds who come to visit them, and who are generally unaware of the history that surrounds them. Burne also wrote: 'I am increasingly aware of the fact that this aspect of our national history has been surprisingly – even shockingly – neglected.'

Although I agree with these sentiments, I have attempted to rectify the problem, as least as far as Wakefield is concerned, with the publication of this work which I hope will be viewed in the years to come as a guide for everyday people to the campaign, battle and battlefield of Wakefield 1460.

In writing this work, I have reviewed – as far as I am aware – all the documentation available on the actual mêlée of the battle and the site of the battlefield itself. In many instances, I have quoted from the authors of other books and journals. I make no apology for this, as many of these earlier writers were – and still are – specialists in their own field, and as such are more qualified than I to make an assessment of a particular aspect of the battle. Therefore, it would be foolish for me to try to compete with them, and even more remiss of me to take their work and words as my own.

List of Illustrations

Acknowledgements

I would like to thank the following people for their help and support in bringing this work to its conclusion. The staff of both Leeds and Wakefield Libraries, for supplying many previously produced, but out of print articles and works regarding the battle of Wakefield – I never cease to be amazed by their patience, knowledge and willingness to help. In respect of this, I would particularly like to thank Ms Jennifer Horne of Leeds Library, without whose efforts on my behalf much of the supporting documentation required to produce this work would have been very difficult and certainly time-consuming to find.

I would also like to thank Simon Axup for taking the time to review the work, and correcting the grammar and improving the text; Graham Shaw, for once again providing the artwork; and my fellow historians Andrew Boardman and Dave Cooke for enlightening me to some facts hitherto unknown to me regarding the battle of Wakefield. On this latter note, I would also like to thank Geoffrey Wheeler for his kind help regarding the content of this work and for the illustrations he supplied. Thanks are also due to the noted battlefield historian and author William Seymour for taking the trouble to read this work and providing me with many useful hints and tips regarding its composition; and Miss Christelle Garcia for providing the translation of Jean de Waurin's chronicle.

I would again like to thank my wife and family for supporting me in my continuing research into fifteenth-century military history, especially my father-in-law, John Claxton, for joining me in walking and exploring the battlefield of Wakefield, and for the many fine photographs that he took of the area on my behalf. I would also like to thank my friends and colleagues – particularly those who have had to suffer my many battlefield theories and opinions during the time we have spent together – for their ongoing support.

Thanks are also due to Christie's of London, in particular Mr David Williams, for supplying the photograph of the Wakefield Sword and granting permission for its use in this work.

Finally, I would like to say a special thank you to Jonathan Falconer at Sutton Publishing. It is my belief that without his support and efforts on my behalf behind the scenes, this work would never have come to fruition.

CHAPTER ONE

Introduction

. . . because he wished to strip the king of his crown . . .

THE ORIGINS OF THE WARS OF THE ROSES

On the morning of 3 March 1452, at Blackheath, near London, two armed forces faced each other prepared to commence battle, a battle which would have been – had it not been averted – the first engagement of the struggles for the throne that would, in later years, become known as the Wars of the Roses. The entire encounter was recorded in the *London Chronicle* as follows:

King Henry VI; a portrait from c. 1518–23 from the Royal Collection, Windsor Castle. (Royal Collection © HM The Queen)

The 30th year of King Henry the Sixth. This year on Wednesday the 16th day of February the king with the lords rode towards the Duke of York for to take him, because he raised people to come down and take the Duke of Somerset; but when the Duke of York heard here of, he took another way and so came towards London. And also soon the king heard here of, he sent letters to the mayor, alderman and commons of London, on St Mathies' day, that they should keep the city and suffer not the Duke of York to come therein; wherefore was made great watch in the city, the which was told the Duke of York, wherefore he left London way and went over Kingston Bridge. And on the Monday after, in the morning they were removed from thence into Kent. And at afternoon the same day the king came to London with his host, and so went into Southwark and lodged at St Mary Overeys. And the Duke of York pitched his field about Dartford with great ordnance. And whilst the king lay still at St Mary Overeys bishops rode between the king and the Duke of York to set them at rest and peace.

But the Duke of York said he would have the Duke of Somerset, or else he would die therefore. And on Wednesday next following [1st March] the king with his host rode to Blackheath, and forth over Shooters Hill to Welling, and there lodged that day and the morrow. And on Thursday at afternoon there was made a pointment between the king and the Duke of York by the means of lords and on the morrow, that was Friday, the king assembled his host on the Blackheath afore noon; and there abode the coming of the Duke of York after pointment made over even. And in the king's host was numbered 20,000 fighting men, and men said the Duke of York had as many with much great stuff and ordnance. And at the last the Duke of York came with forty horse to the king about noon, and obeyed him to his liegance; and with (him) the Earl of Devonshire and the Lord Cobham, the which held the Duke of York and were in host with him. And the king took them to grace and all.[1]

What the chronicle does not tell us, is that when York entered the king's tent, expecting, in accordance with the king's previous promise, to take the Duke of Somerset into his custody, he found the duke standing on the king's right and he himself – not surprisingly – under arrest. York was held prisoner for three months, and it was only after he swore an oath of allegiance at St Paul's Cathedral never to raise arms against the king again, that he was allowed to go free.

To understand why it was that King Henry VI and his realm's most powerful noble, Richard, Duke of York, should face each other in such a manner, we must return to the year 1411. In that year Richard Plantagenet was born to Richard, 5th Earl of Cambridge, and Anne Mortimer. The 5th Earl was the son of Edmund, 1st Duke of York, who was in turn the fourth son of Edward III. If Henry VI had died before 1453, the year of the birth of his son, Edward, Prince of Wales, then Richard would have undoubtedly been crowned King of England; since the death of Henry VI's uncle and heir Humphrey, Duke of Gloucester, who had died in 1447, there was no other noble who could match

Richard's strong claim to the throne at that time. Being so highly placed in the royal household, Richard was destined to play a significant role in the government and politics of England and in England's affairs in France during the later stages of the Hundred Years War. He was appointed Lieutenant of France in 1436. Throughout his service in Europe, he had to pay for the services of his men and finance the army in France from his own personal funds. Although York was a wealthy man in his own right (he was the sole beneficiary of the childless Edmund Mortimer, who had died of plague in Ireland in 1425), his marriage to Cicely Neville in 1438 brought him great wealth. Known as 'The Rose of Raby', Cicely was the daughter of Ralph Neville, Earl of Westmorland, and the sister of Richard Neville, Earl of Salisbury. Thus enriched, York was able, albeit reluctantly, to fund the English army overseas. By the time he left France, York had spent some £38,000 of his own money to maintain English interests in France. To add insult to injury, in 1445 he was replaced as Lieutenant of France by Edmund Beaufort, Duke of Somerset. Henry VI trusted his cousin Somerset more than he did the Duke of York, and it was doubtless on Somerset's advice that Henry VI appointed York to the post of Lieutenant of Ireland, a position that was, in reality, little more than exile by office. This further widened the rift between the two nobles, and Somerset's wariness of York was enhanced when the king forwarded the sum of £25,000 to Somerset to maintain the army in France.

York detested Somerset, partly because he resented the favouritism shown him by the king, but also because Somerset had replaced him as Lieutenant of France – and had been granted royal funds to support his men – despite his inability as a soldier.[2]

York's fears for the success of the campaign in France were soon realized when the war began to go badly for the English. The Duke of Somerset was personally responsible for the surrender of the strategic town of Rouen which subsequently led to the fall of Normandy to Charles VII of France. Because of this defeat, Somerset became distinctly unpopular at home. However, because he retained the king's favour, he maintained his prestigious position at court.

In June 1451 Bordeaux and Gascony were lost to the French. This was disastrous news for the English and Henry VI took the loss very badly. York was quick to blame Somerset for the disaster, and with support for the king and his adherents at such a low point (due mainly to English failings in France), York decided to risk all and attempt to wrest control from the king by force of arms, and arrest the Duke of Somerset, thus removing him from his position as the king's most senior advisor. Doubtless this move was inspired not only by York's fear for the conduct of the war in France, but also because he was equally concerned that Somerset might try to insinuate himself into the position that York felt was rightfully his – as the heir to the throne in the event that Henry VI fathered no children. With this intent, and believing that he had more popular support than was actually the case, York sailed from Ireland and landed in North Wales, where he gathered his forces and travelled straight for London and the encounter at Blackheath.

Henry VI creates John Talbot first Earl of Shrewsbury in 1442, for his services in France, where he served as Lieutenant to Richard Duke of York. (British Library, Royal MS 15 EVI, f. 205)

THE WARS OF THE ROSES BEGIN

After York's release from custody, there then followed several years of relative peace.[3] However, by the year 1453, the political storm clouds were once again gathering over the country. By this time, England's possessions in France had been almost entirely lost and the disastrous Hundred Years War had all but come to an end.[4]

It was this – so it is said – that caused Henry VI's first bout of madness. Exactly what form his illness took is not recorded, but it seems that it manifested itself in a form of paralysis. With the king incapacitated, York was made Protector of England and soon took advantage of his position to seek revenge on his earlier enemies; the Duke of Somerset was sent to the Tower on a revised charge of treason (for his poor management of the war in France) in September 1453.

Richard Neville, Earl of Salisbury, and his eldest son Richard, Earl of Warwick, also took advantage of the opportunity afforded by the king's illness, and, under the cover of their kinsman's Protectorate, began to seek their revenge against the Percy family, Earls of Northumberland, with whom they had held a long-running feud over the issue of ownership of property in Northumberland and Yorkshire.[5]

Richard Duke of York; a stained glass portrait from c. *1460 in Cirencester parish church.*
(G. Wheeler)

Thus England was plunged into a series of skirmishes between the land's most powerful lords. The Duke of York used his authority as Protector to the advantage of his family and supporters. However, this all came to an end when the king recovered from his illness in January 1455 and took control of his realm once again. Somerset was released from the Tower, and immediately formed an alliance with Henry Percy, Earl of Northumberland, and Percy's ally in the north, Lord Clifford, against the Duke of York – who was stripped of his powers as Protector – and his supporters, namely the Earl of Salisbury and the Earl of Warwick. With this the battle lines for the Wars of the Roses were drawn. Somerset, Northumberland and Clifford, supported by the king, would in later years be known as Lancastrians, a name derived from the family name of the House of Lancaster to which Henry VI belonged. The followers of the House of York – Warwick, Salisbury and the Duke of York himself – became known as the Yorkists.[6]

The Duke of York, aware that as soon as he was removed from the office of Protector he would become the target of Lancastrian hostility, returned to his estates in the north to consider what course of action to take. His fears were soon realized when he was asked to attend a council meeting to be held at Leicester on 21 May 1455 – he was instructed to come alone, with no friends or supporters.

'The plucking of the red and white roses, in the Old Temple Gardens', by Henry Payne, immortalizing a scene from Shakespeare, where the opposing factions declare their loyalty by picking either a red rose (for the Lancastrians) or a white rose (for the Yorkists). In reality, the conflict was not known as the Wars of the Roses until many years afterwards, when it was christened as such by Sir Walter Scott in the nineteenth century. (G. Wheeler)

Determined not to be trapped again, the Duke gathered together his forces and those of the Earls of Salisbury and Warwick, and marched south to confront the king. What transpired was chronicled as follows:

When the Duke of Somerset and those who were of his party then being in the City of London, heard that the Duke of York and many other lords in his company were advancing against them with a force of five thousand men and when they considered what he had done against the said Duke of York and that he was also in very bad odour with the people of London, he came to the conclusion that he would fall upon him the moment he [the Duke of York] arrived. For which cause he persuaded the king to sally forth against the Duke of York and his other enemies, their opponents, and hastily gathered the said third day after the feast of Ascension up to 3,500 persons and on the 21st day of May in the morning [they] issued out of London and went to lodge twenty miles away from there at a little village where there is an abbey called St Albans, near the which village at less than half a day's march their enemies were lodged.

These, when they knew of the king's coming, immediately approached him and also the 22nd day of the said month very early the king sent a herald to the Duke of York to know the cause for which he had come there with so many men and that it seemed to the king something quite new that he, the duke, should be rising against him, the king. The reply made was that he was not coming against him thus, [he] was always ready to do him obedience but he well intended in one way or another to have the traitors who were about him so that they should be punished, and that in case he could not have them with good will and fair consent, he intended in any case to have them by force.[7]

With this, the parley ended and the battle began.[8]

The Yorkists attempted to gain access to the fortified town of St Albans by attacking the town gates located on Sopwell Lane and Shropshire Lane. However, it was only an attack by the Earl of Warwick's men, commanded by Sir Robert Ogle, through the 'Back Gardens', the piece of ground located between the aforementioned gates, that broke the deadlock; the battle ended with the defeat of the Lancastrians, the capture of the king, and the deaths of Henry Percy, Earl of Northumberland, Edmund Beaufort, Duke of Somerset, and Lord Clifford of Craven.

The king, having been captured during the battle and now enjoying the 'protection' of his Yorkist cousins, returned to London the next day and entered the city with great pomp and ceremony. York rode on his right, the Earl of Salisbury on his left, while the Earl of Warwick rode a little ahead bearing the royal sword. Having achieved this 'coup', the Duke of York was again made Protector of the realm. However, this came to an end in February 1456, when the king, no doubt inspired by the tenacious nature of his wife, Margaret of Anjou, announced that he was able to rule in his own right; he threw off the shackles of his Yorkist adversaries and set about trying to re-impose his rule over the kingdom.

In reality, Margaret of Anjou was the main fomenter of the Lancastrian resurgence, and it was she who instigated, in Henry's name, the removal of all Yorkist supporters from offices of state, to which they had been appointed by the Duke of York during his time in office as Protector. At this, the Duke of York and the Earl of Salisbury once again retreated to their estates in the north. The queen, determined to rid herself and her husband of Yorkist undertones once and for all, arranged for a council meeting to be held at Coventry in June 1459. All the great nobles were commanded to attend this meeting. However, York, Salisbury and

Warwick (recently returned from Calais) were not invited, and Margaret planned to have them all charged with acts of treason against the king and the state.

York, realizing what was at stake, organized his forces and sent word to the Earl of Salisbury, then at Middleham, and the Earl of Warwick, then in London, to meet with him near York's stronghold at Ludlow. The Lancastrians, however, were not unaware of what the Duke was planning and several moves were made to intercept them. Only one force, under the command of John Touchet, Lord Audley, was successful in achieving this, however; on 23 September 1459 his army came across the forces of the Earl of Salisbury at Blore Heath, near Newcastle under Lyme.[9]

The Yorkists were the victors in the battle that was fought that day, and a short while later they managed to join together with York and Warwick at Ludford Bridge near Ludlow, but it was here that treachery was first to show its hand. A contingent of the Earl of Warwick's men, under the command of Andrew Trollope, their captain, acting on a promise of pardon given by Henry VI, deserted to the Lancastrians, causing the remaining Yorkist commanders to lose heart. It was a serious loss, and faced with such overwhelming opposition the Yorkist leaders were forced to plan their escape. Under the pretence of returning to Ludlow Castle for the night, the Yorkist commanders fled. The Duke of York, taking the Earl of Rutland with him, returned to the safety of Ireland while the Earl of Warwick, Earl of Salisbury and Edward, Earl of March, fled to the safety of Calais.[10]

With this, it appeared that the Yorkist cause had come to an end, especially after the Yorkist commanders were formally 'attainted' and declared traitors at a Parliament held at Coventry in November. However, the Lancastrians did not reckon with the tenacity and courage of the Earl of Warwick, whose actions in the coming months were to turn the fortunes of the wars once again, this time in the Yorkists' favour. Although 'trapped' in Calais, the Earl of Warwick, who was as much at home at sea as he was on dry land, was soon conducting pirate-style raids on passing shipping, as well as planning the revival of the Yorkist cause on mainland England. To assist with this, Warwick sailed to Ireland in March 1460 to confer with the Duke of York and plan the Yorkist return to power. Calais, which he had left under the command of the Earls of Salisbury and March, was soon placed under siege by a Lancastrian force under the command of Henry Beaufort, Edmund's son, who was now the Duke of Somerset. However, the fortress remained resolute, and the Duke of Somerset had to withdraw to the nearby fortress of Guines.

When Warwick returned to Calais in May 1460, it appears that the Yorkists plans for the 'invasion' of England were complete. On 26 June 1460 the Earl of Warwick, together with the Earls of Salisbury and March, landed at Sandwich with a small army and proceeded to march for London. Their small force was soon joined by many followers from Kent, where the Yorkist commanders had remained popular, and soon reached the capital. Meanwhile, the Lancastrians were gathering at Coventry and Warwick.

The Earl of Warwick, his army increasing in numbers all the time, was eager to bring his enemy into battle. The two forces met at Northampton on 10 July 1460.

Henry VI (left) watches as Edward Earl of March and the Earls of Salisbury and Warwick flee England by boat for the safety of Calais, after the Yorkist campaign of 1459 which opened favourably with a victory at the battle of Blore Heath, but ended disastrously at Ludford Bridge. From the contemporary illustrated Chronicle Roll 'Life of Edward IV'. (British Library, Harley MS 7353)

The battle that followed was described by the author of *An English Chronicle of the reigns of Richard II, Henry IV, V, VI* as follows:

The king at Northampton lay at Friars and had ordained there a strong and a mighty field, in the meadows beside the nunnery, armed and arrayed with guns, having the river at his back. The earls with the number of 60,000, as it was said, came to Northampton and sent certain bishops to the king beseeching him that in eschewing of effusion of Christian blood he would admit and suffer the earls to come to his presence to declare them self as they were.

The Duke of Buckingham that stood beside the king, said unto them, 'Ye come not as Bishops for to treat for peace, but as men of arms'; because they brought with them a notable company of men at arms. They answered and said, 'We come thus for surety of our persons, for they that be-eth about the king be-eth not our friends.' 'Forsooth,' said the duke, 'the Earl of Warwick shall not come to the king's presence, and if he come he shall die.' The messengers returned again, and told this to the earls . . .

Then on the Thursday the 10th of July, the year of Our Lord 1460, at two hours after noon, the said Earls of March and Warwick let cry through the field, that no man should lay a hand on the king ne on the common people, but only on the lords, knights and squires: then trumpets blew up, and both hosts countered and fought together half an hour. The Lord Grey, that was the king's vaward, broke the field and came to the earl's [Warwick and Edward's] party which caused the salvation of many a man's life: many were slain, and many were fled, and were drowned in the river.[11]

With this, the battle ended and the Lancastrian rout began.[12]

THE ACT OF ACCORD

King Henry, who was captured after the battle, found himself once more under the 'protection' of the Yorkists, and the Earl of Warwick immediately ordered a return to London so that the Yorkist commanders could once again set about establishing their control over the realm. Throughout this period, the Duke of York had remained in Ireland. However, early in September he landed at Chester and made a leisurely tour of the Welsh Marches before travelling to London. Upon his arrival in the capital, York ordered that trumpets be sounded and that his sword should be held before him as he marched to Westminster, where many of the lords of the land had gathered to await his arrival. Abbot Whethamstede of St Albans abbey takes up the story:

And coming there he walked straight on, until he came to the king's throne, upon the covering or cushion on which laying his hand, in this very act like a man about to take possession of his right, he held it upon it for a short time. But at length withdrawing it, he turned his face to the people; standing quietly under the canopy of royal state, he looked eagerly for their applause.

While however, he was standing thus and turning his face to the people and while he was judging their applause, Master Thomas Bourchier, Archbishop of Canterbury, rose up and having exchanged greetings asked if he would come and see the king. He [York], as if stung in soul by this question, replied shortly: 'I do not recall that I know anyone within the kingdom whom it would not befit to come sooner to me and see me rather than I should go visit him.'

The archbishop having heard this reply, quickly withdrew, and reported to the king, the answer which he had heard from the duke's mouth. While the archbishop was thus withdrawing, he too retired to the principal apartments of the whole palace.[13]

It is clear that the Duke had, until this point, believed that he had the overwhelming support of the lords and nobles who were present. However, as Abbot Whethamstede's quotation clearly demonstrates, York had once again failed to comprehend the reality of the political situation and had overestimated the level of support he actually had. The probable explanation for this was that the lords were disillusioned with York's having remained in Ireland for so long, leaving the Earl of Warwick to lead the Yorkist campaign in England. Moreover, it is likely that the lords and nobles of the land, although despairing at Henry VI's weak rule, were nevertheless all too aware that Henry was their anointed king. Supporting York's claim to the throne, though no doubt an appealing idea to many, would require them to break their sworn oaths of fealty to the king; it would also require the Duke of York and the Earl of Warwick to break their oaths never again to take up arms against the king. Little wonder the lords hesitated – in a chivalrous age, this action went far beyond what they felt they could openly support with honour.

The Earl of Warwick, it appears, was aware of the lords' reluctance and as Jean de Waurin later related, was furious with the Duke of York. Shortly after this debacle, he went to the duke 'and there were angry words, for the earl showed the duke how the lords and people were ill content against him because he wished to strip the king of his crown'.[14]

Instead they soon set about pressing home York's claim to rule the country by legal means. To that end, in a meeting of the Lords and the Commons on 7 October, Parliament recognized York's position, and on 24 October passed the Act of Accord, by which it was agreed that Henry would remain king until his death, whereupon the crown would pass to the Duke of York or his heirs.[15]

Clearly, the 'Act of Accord' was a direct result of the Lancastrian defeat at the battle of Northampton. This point was not lost on the modern-day historian, Anthony Goodman, who wrote in *The Wars of the Roses*:

> The consequences of the battle of Northampton differed greatly from those of the first battle of St Albans. The latter had so shocked contemporaries that it has ushered in a period of political compromise, leading eventually to the new court ascendancy against which York rebelled in 1459. But the compromise after Northampton rested on a novel, even more unstable basis – the recognition of Yorkist dynastic claims. York's acceptance as Henry's heir in the Parliament in October immediately provoked a struggle for the crown, a war of succession, producing widespread involvement and lasting bitterness as it developed into what some contemporaries regarded as a war of the north against the south. Once the dynastic issue had been raised, with such dramatic and extreme consequences, it was hard to bottle up again.[16]

As such, further conflict was inevitable.

CHAPTER TWO

The Wakefield Campaign – 1460

. . . by dint of swoorde, and for that cause . . .

THE MARCH FROM LONDON

The reason for the claim that the Act of Accord, ratified on 24 October 1460, brought about the battle of Wakefield is as follows. Although this constitutional settlement was acceptable to the Yorkists, it certainly did not sit well with the Lancastrians. Queen Margaret in particular was opposed to it, because it effectively prevented her own son, Prince Edward, from taking the throne of England. However, with the king held under the 'protection' of his Yorkist cousins, Margaret's options were limited. But she was not one to sit idly by and allow the Yorkists to have it all their own way; instead she set about planning the 'liberation' of the king. Her first action was to send word to her adherents in the North, particularly the Earl of Northumberland and Lord Clifford,[1] plus several other staunch Lancastrians, to make ready for the forthcoming armed struggle. This action was chronicled by William Gregory who wrote:

> Then the queen having knowledge of this party while she sent unto the Duke of Somerset, at that time being in Dorsetshire at the castle of Corfe, and for the Earl of Devonshire, and for Alexander Hody, and prayed them to come to her hastily as they might, with their tenants as strong in their harness to war, for the Lord Roos, the Lord Clifford, the Baron of Greystock, the Lord Neville, the Lord Latimer, were waiting upon the Duke of Exeter to meet with her in Hull. And this matter was not tarried but full privily i-wrought; and she sent letters unto all her chief officers that they would do the same, and that they should warn all who [were] servants that loved her or purposed to keep or rejoice their office, to wait upon her at Hull by that day as it [was] appointed by her. All these people gathered and conveyed so privily that they were whole in number of 15,000 ere any man would believe it; in so much if any man said, or told, or talked of such gathering, he should be schende [disgraced], and some were in great danger, for the common people said by thoo that told the truth,

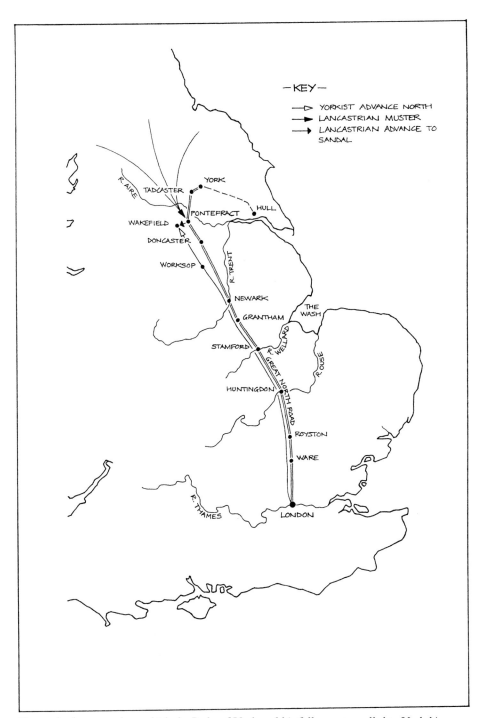

Figure A: the route along which the Duke of York and his followers travelled to Yorkshire.

'Ye talk right ye would it were', and given no credence of their saying. But last the lords proposed to know the truth.[2]

Hall, in his account, is more vocal, and in his chronicle he hints at what he believed the queen's plans were:

> The Duke of York well knowing that the queen would spurn and impugne the conclusions agreed and taken in this parliament [the Act of Accord], caused her and her son to be sent for by the king; but she being a manly woman, wishing to rule and not be ruled, & there to counselled by the Dukes of Exeter and Somerset, not only denied to come, but also assembled together a great army, intending to take the king by fine force, out of the lords' hands, and set them to a new school. The protector lying in London, having perfect knowledge of all these doings . . .[3]

Although the chronicler Gregory wrote that Hull was the muster point, I believe he was mistaken. It is clear that the meeting point was actually planned to be at the Lancastrian stronghold of Pontefract, deep in the Lancastrian heartland of Yorkshire. However, this is not everybody's point of view. Goodman, in his own book, *The Wars of the Roses*, suggested Hull was the muster point, primarily because the Lancastrians needed the port facilities provided by Hull to help provide the growing army with sufficient supplies. This view is shared by P.A. Johnson in *Duke Richard Of York 1411–1460*, p. 219. My own view is that there was sufficient support from the surrounding countryside for the Lancastrians to ensure adequate supplies were provided for their army. One possible explanation has been offered for this confusion: the fact that Margaret was actually in Hull when she wrote the letters to her adherents summoning them to arms may simply have misled the chronicler Gregory into believing that Hull would be the muster point. It has also been suggested that at the same time she wrote to her Welsh allies in order to bring about their support, and that once this was completed she then took ship to Scotland.

My own view is that this is not the case, and that the facts are as follows. After writing her letters from Hull, Margaret's second task was to travel to Wales in person in order to enlist the support of Jasper Tudor, Earl of Pembroke, and his father Owen Tudor,[4] King Henry VI's stepfather – both staunch Lancastrians – against the Yorkists.

It is claimed that on her travels to Wales, her small contingent was set upon by men under the command of Thomas, Lord Stanley. However, she and her son managed to escape and complete their journey to Wales. Later, when she had done all she could to raise support for the Lancastrian cause in Wales, she boarded a ship bound for Scotland in an effort to enlist Scottish support and to raise a mercenary army to supplement the Lancastrian forces already gathering in England. The Yorkists, meanwhile, must by now have been aware of Margaret's activities, although there is scant evidence to suggest they knew she was heading for Scotland.[5] Their response to Margaret's opening moves was chronicled as follows:

After these things the Duke of York, knowing for certaine that the queen would not be content with the decree of this parliament [appointing him successor to the crown] made speede into Yorkshire to pursue her . . .

. . . Likewise the queen, who was resolved in minde to demand her husbande by dint of swoorde, and for that cause had alreadie assembled a puissant armie, against them.[6]

Autumn passed into winter and the Lancastrian strength grew, their muster being an exceptionally large one, and it was no mean feat when one considers the time of year. It is perhaps testament to the general feeling of resentment towards the Yorkists, and particularly the Act of Accord, that so many flocked to the Lancastrian banners.

In the meanwhile, the Yorkist plans to counteract the Lancastrians were almost complete. The Duke intended to march north to deal with the Lancastrians in person, an action which was rapidly becoming increasingly necessary, not only to counter the Lancastrian forces gathering in the North and protect the northern fortress, but also to protect his Yorkshire tenants. York certainly took the threat seriously – he even made out his will before travelling north. (With the benefit of hindsight, it is easy to say that this was perhaps a bad omen, bearing in mind the

Margaret of Anjou, from a drawing of a window that used to be in the Church of the Cordeliers, Angers. Margaret's determination, in the face of the Act of Accord and strong Yorkist opposition, kept the Lancastrian cause alive during the late 1450s and early 1460s. (G. Wheeler)

result of the coming campaign.) He also commissioned his eldest son Edward, Earl of March, in his first independent command, and ordered him to follow in Margaret's footsteps and put down the growing rebellion against the Yorkists in Wales. However, due to the fact that York had so few supporters in the North, Edward was ordered to follow on to Yorkshire as soon as possible, to assist his father in suppressing the Lancastrians.

The county of Yorkshire was predominantly Lancastrian, and the few Yorkist tenants present were mainly congregated in the South (West Riding); and were already suffering greatly at the hands of the marauding Lancastrians, in the absence of an effective Yorkist power in the North. Indeed, the chronicler William of Worcester reported that while the Lancastrians plundered their villages and farmsteads, many of the Duke's followers and tenants were forced at swordpoint to join the Lancastrians – or face the consequences.

At the same time the Duke of York gave a commission to the Earl of Warwick to remain in London to 'protect' the king, as the following chronicle shows:

> The Duke of York protector being at London,[7] assigned the Duke of Norfolk and the Earl of Warwick his trusted friends, to be about the king, and he with the Earl of Salisbury and the Earl of Rutland, and a convenient number of men, departed out of London, the second of December, and sent to the Earl of March his eldest son to follow him with all his power.[8]

Amid all the lengthy preparations, parliament was called; Warwick's brother, George Neville, Bishop of Exeter, opened the proceedings with a rousing speech in which he likened the Yorkist cause to a religious crusade. The context of his words were not lost on the modern historian P.A. Johnson, who wrote:

> When Bishop Neville opened parliament, he chose as his text lines from the prophet Joel; in the circumstances a shrewd choice. The prophet's call was for repentance, self-sacrifice, and unity of purpose in the face of an invading army, the invader from the north . . .
>
> The decision to go north, implicit in Neville's sermon, was not an easy one to take in November. Some at least thought Queen Margaret to be in Wales with the Earl of Pembroke, robbed of her cash, but confident of reinforcements. They were wrong, as York and his advisors may have known, but even had she not been in the north there was an urgent need to intervene there as quickly as possible, partly to prevent vital castles being handed over to the Scots or the queen, or both, partly to restore order before the trouble could spill south. This was not just a problem of localised rioting. The Earl of Northumberland was actively constructing an army in Yorkshire, ordering all men aged between sixteen and sixty to enlist to rescue the king . . .[9]

Clearly, the Duke of York realized that the heart of the Lancastrian strength lay in the northern counties; he also knew that his arrival in Yorkshire would not be celebrated by the local people. The author of *An English Chronicle of the reigns of Richard II, Henry IV, V, VI* wrote:

. . . and anon after the said Duke of York, the Earl of Rutland his son, and the Earl of Salisbury, a little before Christmas, with a few persons went in to the north also, for to repress the malaice of the northern men the which loved not the said Duke of York ne the Earl of Salisbury.[10]

The Duke left London on 2 December, although some believe he did not leave the capital until the 9th, a week later. Markham (p. 110), Brooke (p. 53), Leadman (p. 353) and Stansfield (p. 26), all agree that the Duke of York left London on the 2nd; in contrast, Gillingham in his book *The Wars of the Roses* (Weidenfield, 1981, p. 119), and Ross in *Edward IV* (p. 30), state that the Duke left on the 9th. Even the chroniclers disagree – Hall (p. 250) says the 2nd, while Gregory (p. 208) says the 9th. Some do not give a date at all, merely describing the departure. According to the Abbot of St Albans abbey, Duke Richard:

set out towards the north, and there set out with him the illustrious and notable Lord Richard Neville Earl of Salisbury. Journeying together they gathered a great force of people as they went, by authority of a royal commission, as protection for there own persons and to put down and repress the multitude of their adversaries.[11]

Engraving of Baynard's Castle, the London residence of the Duke of York. It was from here between 2 and 9 December that the Duke and his son Edmund Earl of Rutland and their supporters left London to begin their fateful journey into Yorkshire. (G. Wheeler)

This is also recorded by William of Worcester who states:

> Parliament being prorogued in December, the duke and earl [York and Salisbury] hastened from London with a large armed force towards York.[12]

The chosen route of the Duke and his followers was initially along the Great North Road (see figure A). Although the organization of the Duke's forces is not recorded, he would have travelled in the customary three wards, vanguard, middle and rearguard. One must assume that he expected to find provisions and supplies along the way and, as a result the Yorkist baggage train would have been quite small. However, there appears to be some confusion over the size of the Duke's baggage and artillery train. The author of *An English Chronicle of the reigns of Richard II, Henry IV, V, VI* (pp. 106–7), implies that there was 'a great ordnance of guns and other stuffs of war', in the Duke's retinue. By contrast, Goodman, in his book *The Wars of the Roses* (p. 42), claims that the Duke left with only a few hundred followers, and Salisbury with less than a hundred, and therefore they were forced to recruit on the way. Boardman, in *The Battle of Towton* (p. 26), claims that the artillery was forced to turn back due to bad weather – a suggestion reinforced by the fact that no artillery was involved in the battle of Wakefield. Gillingham, in *The Wars of the Roses* (p. 119), claims that the Duke left with a force of 6,000 men.

Clearly, there is no continuity regarding the whole issue of York's march north. Even the contemporary and near-contemporary chroniclers differ, their only points of agreement being that the Yorkist forces met the Lancastrians at Worksop, and that they arrived at Sandal sometime between 21 and 24 December.

THE ENCOUNTER AT WORKSOP

At about the same time as the Duke of York was leaving London, the Duke of Somerset was also travelling north from his castle at Corfe. Having previously been in France trying to break the Yorkist hold on the fortress and Port of Calais, he had been delayed in reaching the muster point; he was now hurrying northwards with the Earl of Devon and several other Lancastrians. All the chroniclers agree that Somerset's force clashed with elements of the Yorkist vanguard at or near Worksop. William of Worcester wrote that the army of the Duke of York:

> . . . coming unexpectedly upon the troops of the Duke of Somerset at Worksop, their vanguard [the Yorkists] was destroyed.[13]

Little is known about this encounter, even the date when it took place. However, it seems unlikely that the Duke of York's entire vanguard was totally destroyed as Worcester suggests. The reason for this is that it is doubtful that this was a planned encounter. Indeed, the words of the chronicle indicates that the Yorkist vanguard, or at least elements of it, probably the mounted forerunners, scouts and so on, came across the Lancastrians, and not the other way around. Unprepared for battle, and facing superior numbers of Lancastrians, it is probable that the Yorkists came off the worse in the skirmish, although the Yorkist numbers involved would have been very small in the first place. Somerset, thus made aware of the Yorkist advance and conscious that York's approaching army probably outnumbered his own, swiftly ordered his men on towards Pontefract before the main Yorkist army could fall upon him, now that his location was known to them.

The Duke of York's intended destination in Yorkshire is still not clear today. His initial plan, before he became aware of the Lancastrian strength, was to travel directly up the Great North Road to Pontefract and confront the Lancastrians directly.[14]

However, Worksop is not located on the Great North Road, and therefore something must have occurred to make the Yorkists change direction. I suggest the following. It could be argued that after the artillery had been forced by bad weather to return to London, and perhaps even before the encounter at Worksop, the Duke, advised by his many councillors and probably working from more recent intelligence, had already realised that the Lancastrian strength was in actual fact much greater than he had originally anticipated. As such, he may have concluded that the current strength of his army would have been insufficient either to force a siege at Pontefract or face the Lancastrians in open battle.

At this point it would seem likely that the Duke and his advisors sought another destination where they could await the arrival of reinforcements (particularly the men under the command of the Earl of March, then heading toward Wales), before travelling to Pontefract to confront the Lancastrians. Therefore, they chose to leave the Great North Road and head towards the Duke's castle at Sandal.

THE ARRIVAL AT SANDAL

Apart from the encounter at Worksop, it appears that the rest of the journey was accomplished without incident, and the Duke and his army arrived at Sandal sometime between 21 and 24 December. Worcester's chronicle records the duke's arrival thus:

> On the 21st of December, however, they reached Sandal Castle, with 6,000 men . . .[15]

Edward Hall, in contrast, chronicled the Duke's arrival as follows:

> The duke by small journeys, came to his castle of Sandal, besides Wakefield, on Christmas Eve, and there began to assemble his tenants and friends.[16]

And Stow as follows:

> The duke came to the castle of Sandal besides Wakefield on Christmas Eve, and there began to assemble his tenants and friends.[17]

Pontefract Castle, a seventeenth-century painting by Alexander Kiernick. The castle was the muster point for the Lancastrian army before the battle of Wakefield. It was with the intention of recapturing the northern fortresses such as Pontefract, as well as to protect his northern tenants from Lancastrian retribution, that the Duke of York marched into Yorkshire in December 1460. (G. Wheeler)

Christmas appears to have come and gone without incident, and it seems that the Duke of York celebrated Christmas peacefully at Sandal despite being short of supplies. In the words of the chroniclers:

> . . . and kept their Christmas there, notwithstanding that the enemy under the Duke of Somerset and the Earl of Northumberland, were close by at Pontefract.[18]

It has been suggested that the Yorkists and the Lancastrians agreed on a Christmas truce, a truce which is said to have been negotiated directly between the Duke of York and the Duke of Somerset. It was supposed to last from some unrecorded time before Christmas until Epiphany – 6 January. Although this is mentioned by some modern-day historians,[19] it is not recorded by any of the contemporary or near-contemporary chroniclers save one.[20] As such, in my opinion, it has, to be viewed at best with caution, and at worst as having no basis in fact.

It must have been a desperate time for the Duke of York; isolated in his castle, short of both supplies and reinforcements, he believed that his enemy faced him in overwhelming numbers. Even his attempts to recruit locally had failed, as the chronicler de Waurin noted:

The Duke of York, who was then staying in Wakefield, hearing that the Queen Margaret was coming with the Duke of Somerset and a large group of armed men in order to fight, was as such concerned for at that time he did not have enough people to resist against such a demonstration of force. He talked with the Earl of Salisbury and all the people on his side to review their situation and tried to get people from everywhere in an attempt to increase their strength and power within the town [castle], but all this did not suffice as at that time most of the people were out in the fields.[21]

Therefore, the Yorkists at Sandal and the Lancastrians 9 miles away at Pontefract celebrated their Christmas in the perfect knowledge of each other's presence – and no doubt planning how best to bring about each other's demise.

CHAPTER THREE

A Brief History of Sandal Castle

. . . thou never saw me keep fortress . . .

THE OWNERS OF THE CASTLE

According to Lawrence Butler (on whose work *Sandal Castle, Wakefield*, published in 1991 by Wakefield Historical Publications, this chapter is largely based), it was the building of the great earth mound and the digging of the wide trenches in Norman times that marked the beginnings of a fortification at Sandal, Wakefield.

Although there is evidence of earlier occupation within the surrounding areas, dating to before the Roman invasion of Britain, it is generally accepted that it was a member of the Warenne family – although there is no evidence to pinpoint the individual – who ordered the castle's construction. It appears that the manor of Wakefield came into the possession of William de Warenne, 2nd Earl of Surrey, some time between 1106 and 1121. The change in ownership of the manor when Warenne took possession, coupled with the requirement for an administrative centre for the area, brought about the need for the construction of a castle.

The Warenne family originated in Normandy and Picardy, where they held lands. William de Warenne rose rapidly to prominence at the court of Duke William of Normandy, mainly due to his skills in combat. Because of his ability in military matters, it appears that he was an important figure in the conquest of England in 1066. He was rewarded by being given the title Earl of Surrey and was granted several manors scattered throughout England, notably in Norfolk, Surrey and Sussex. The extensive manor of Sandal was granted to William's son, the 2nd Earl, perhaps as a reward for the part that he played in Henry I's conquest of Normandy, especially in the crucial battle of Tinchebrai in 1106.

The Warenne family maintained ownership of the manor and castle of Sandal until the death of John, the 8th Earl of Surrey, in 1347. At this time the manor of Wakefield reverted to the Crown, and King Edward III granted it to his fourth son, Edmund of Langley, who in 1362 was to become the Earl of Cambridge. Although the earl played only a minor role at the court of Edward III, during the

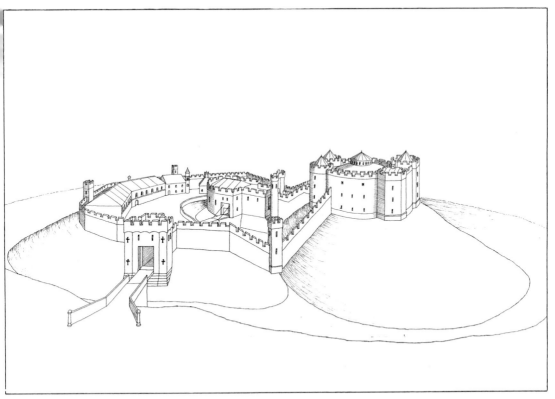

Reconstruction of Sandal Castle by Graham Shaw, showing how it may have looked in the fifteenth century. Although an impressive sight in its heyday, Sandal Castle was a relatively small fortress compared to Pontefract, Dunstanburgh and other northern castles. (Author's collection)

reign of Edward's grandson Richard II, he played an important role in suppressing the increasing trouble in France, campaigning regularly not only in France but in Portugal as well. In recognition of his support, the king created him Duke of York in 1385, and in the later years of Richard's reign he acted as regent on three separate occasions.

Although Edmund died in 1402, the manor of Wakefield remained the property of the Dukes of York for a long time after this date. So it was that Richard, Duke of York, inherited the castle in 1415. After his death, his eldest son inherited the title, and thus the family retained ownership of the castle. Indeed, it stayed in the hands of the Dukes of York or the Crown (as the Duke of York) until the year 1566.

Richard III's death at Bosworth in 1485 brought an end to Sandal Castle's role as a royal residence.[1] Although the upkeep of the castle was maintained, it remained an administrative centre until the time of Henry VIII, when the manor

Tomb effigy of Sir John Savile (d. 1492), Thornhill, Yorkshire. The Savile family leased Sandal estate from the crown in 1586, and retained it until 1638, when the estate was sold to the family of Francis Nevile. (G. Wheeler)

courts, which were held every three weeks, were moved to Moot Hall. After this, the castle was leased to several individuals throughout the sixteenth and seventeenth centuries: in 1556 it was leased to Edward Carey and remained in his possession until 1586 when it passed to Sir John Savile, who retained the lease until 1619. After this date it was leased to Sir Thomas Savile, who held possession of the castle until it was sold by the Crown to Francis Nevile in 1638.

Whatever plans Francis Nevile may have had for the castle, they certainly never came to fruition, for they were no doubt overtaken by the events of the English Civil War. Major Thomas Beaumont of Whitley instructed that a Royalist garrison be installed at Sandal Castle, under the command of Major Ward. But Ward's command was shortlived, for he slipped on one of the stone staircases at the castle and broke his neck. His replacement was Colonel George Bonivant, who stayed in command of the castle throughout the remainder of the Civil War. The castle was besieged by Parliament in 1645, when Thomas Fairfax ordered Sir John Savile of Lupset to take command of the force sent to lay siege to the castle.

When the castle was finally given over to the forces of Parliament, the order was given to destroy totally what had not been ruined by cannon fire during the siege itself. Thus the castle, or what remained of it, was totally destroyed.

Contemporary pew end from Sandal Magna Church, which shows the coats of arms of a number of past owners of the Sandal Estate. (Author's collection)

In 1765 ownership of the site of the castle passed from the Neviles to the Pilkingtons, a local family of some substance. When Sir Lionel Pilkington bought the Chevet estate from the Neviles – by which he also gained the castle at Sandal – he also gained the private chapel which forms the north transept of St Helen's Church at Sandal. This chapel was previously owned and used by all the lords of the manor, including the Dukes of York, and their coats of arms can be clearly seen carved on an oak panel which is now free-standing at the east end of the church. The chapel remained in the possession of the Pilkington family for nearly 200 years, unlike the castle, which from 1912 was leased to Wakefield Corporation. In 1954 the castle was bought by the people of the city of Wakefield.

Dr J.W. Walker, whose interest in the castle produced the first serious study of the ruins (*see* Chapter 8), was also Sir Lionel Pilkington's family doctor. His interest in the castle and the extensive Pilkington family tree which appears in his book, was no doubt inspired by his association with the family.

THE CASTLE'S CONSTRUCTION

Having established the owners of the castle from its creation through to modern times, we shall now explore the construction of its fortifications. The wide moat

Sandal Castle from an Elizabethan drawing 'Duchy of Lancaster Maps and Plans 1562–4'
(PRO MR16). Compare the likeness to the reconstruction on page 23.

and tall mounds created during early Norman times were, doubtless, crowned
with wooden buildings and timber-based fortifying walls. It seems that it was only
when the castle came into the possession of the 6th Earl of Surrey, yet another
William de Warenne, that the construction of a stone fortress began. The first
stone building in the castle was a flint-built hall located on top of the western
mound. This was soon followed by a series of developments described by Butler
as follows:

> . . . the keep was then built to a plan using half of the intended area. It was
> completed as a structure 79 feet by 40 feet and probably stood to at least 50
> feet high. It was additionally approached through a strongly constructed
> gatehouse set in the encircling perimeter wall. All this was accomplished
> before 1160. No further changes were made to the keep in the late twelfth
> century, and the main scene of building operations moved to the more
> spacious bailey or lower ward where the principal domestic quarters appear to
> have been situated . . .[2]

During the following years, extensive building work continued at the castle and it is unlikely, as Butler points out, that the castle acted as a residence for the Warenne family during this time. They probably stayed in neighbouring castles such as Conisbrough when they visited this part of the country. It appears that the gatehouse block of the keep was the next area of the castle to be improved and when completed was an 'impressive development'. It was followed by improvements to the buildings and defences within the bailey area. Butler wrote:

> Although the overall plan had probably been determined by William, the 6th Earl, the campaign of rebuilding had to be accomplished gradually. The earliest work was the replacement of the gatehouse and timber bridge by a solid outer ramp leading to the drawbridge. Simultaneously with this work was the recutting of the ditch at the base of the motte on its western side and the dumping of the upcast rubble onto the nearest part of the bailey to heighten its surface. The approach to the motte and to the keep built upon it was along a tongue of rock, later protected behind stone built walls.[3]

The later stages of the improvements called for the construction of a curtain wall to replace the timber palisade on top of the bailey bank; it also connected the stone gatehouse to the keep and encircled the entire series of outer dwellings situated on the western bailey. This, along with the construction of some stone buildings within the bailey itself, resulted in the formidable, if comparatively small, Sandal Castle, through whose familiar gates, some time between 21 and 24 December 1460, entered Richard, Duke of York, for the last time.

CHAPTER FOUR

The Battlefield – Past

. . . in the plain ground between his castle and the town . . .

It is impossible now to describe with any degree of accuracy the topography of the battlefield as it appeared in 1460. But the battle is not forgotten – its legacy survives in the street names evident in the surrounding areas, such as Duke of York Avenue, Rutland Avenue and Clifford Avenue which are to be found in the housing estate north-west of the castle.

There are many clues as to the topography of the battlefield in the text of the chroniclers and later historians, who viewed the battlefield before twentieth-century developments destroyed it forever. For example, Richard Brooke was able to view the battlefield in the 1850s before the site was 'developed'. His work, titled *Visits to the Fields of Battle* (John Russell Smith, 1857), is full of geographical descriptions of the battlefield. David Smurthwaite, in *The Complete Guide to the Battlefields of Britain*, is one of the few battlefield historians to include a map of the battlefield in his description of the battle. His map is actually based on the modern Ordnance Survey map of the site, and for those who are unfamiliar with the battlefield today, it gives an excellent demonstration of just how 'developed' the site has become.

Before we begin to explore the movements of the two forces on the field of battle, we first have to agree on where it was fought. There are two schools of thought on this subject. Smurthwaite is a member of what we will call School A. He believes that the Lancastrian front was located to the north-west of the castle, on a stretch of ground which is today partially covered with a man-made lake, with its rear to the meander loop in the River Calder. This suggests that the battle was fought on the stretch of land between the Calder to the north-west of the castle, and the fortress itself (*see* Figure B). Others who agree with him include Freeman (p. 282), and Leadman[1] (p. 354). They hold this opinion despite the evidence from several chroniclers, notably Hall and Vergil, who wrote that the battle was fought 'in the plain ground between his castle and the town of Wakefield'.

If we assume that the evidence of the battle found at Portobello House (*see* pp. 92–3) is an indication of where the battle was fought, then this supports School A's opinion. The site of the house would have been close to the left flank of the Lancastrian front, and therefore not out of place with the facts if we ignore the words of the chroniclers. However, if we take a moment to ponder this

A view of the battlefield as described by the advocates of School A. (Author's collection)

location, and apply what Alfred Burne called IMP (Inherent Military Probability),[2] then on closer scrutiny the argument for the location favoured by School A does not, in my opinion, hold water.

The application of IMP raises the following issues:

1. Is it likely that the Lancastrians would line up for a battle with their rear on the banks of the River Calder? From a military point of view, this would afford no opportunity for manoeuvre if the battle went against them. They would not have forgotten the disaster at Northampton only the previous year, when the Lancastrian defensive position along the banks of the River Nene was overrun, with appalling consequences.

2. If, as we believe, the Lancastrians travelled from Pontefract to the battle-field, then surely they would have approached from the east of the castle. This means they would have had to march directly across the Yorkists' line of fire to reach a position to the north-west of the castle. Would they have done so?

3. If the Lancastrians were attempting to interfere with the Yorkist supply lines, would they have left 'open' the road from Sandal to Wakefield? If they had taken up the position suggested by School A then they would have done.

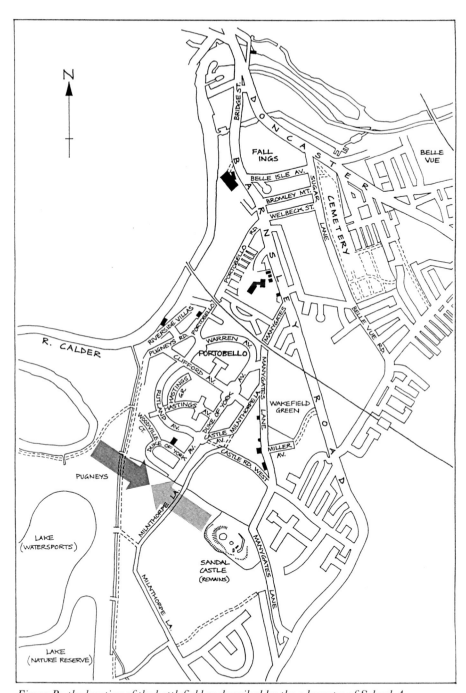

Figure B: the location of the battlefield as described by the advocates of School A.

A view of Sandal Castle from the Lancastrian position as described by the advocates of School A. (Author's collection)

My view is that the answer to all these questions is a resounding No, which brings us to School B's answer to the question of where the battle was fought. We are fortunate to be able to refer to the work of Richard Brooke, who, unlike Burne, actually visited the battlefield and made the following observations:

> On the 31st of July, 1852, I first visited the field of battle, the castle, and also the village and church of Sandal . . . looking from Sandal Castle Hill, a flat plain appears, of considerable extent, cultivated as meadow fields, extending from the castle to the River Calder. These meadows are called 'the Pugnays' . . . adjoining the tract of meadow land is 'Porto Bello', a mansion erected by Samuel Holdsworth, Esq., and now occupied by William Shaw, Esq . . .
>   . . . The battle was fought upon that spot and upon the tract of ground formerly part of Wakefield Green, extending from thence across the turnpike road in a north-eastwardly direction. The green must have been on the southward side of the river, and about half a mile from the bridge; its site is crossed by the modern turnpike road, from Wakefield to Barnsley, and part of it has acquired the name Fall Ings, according to tradition, from great numbers who fell there, in the battle. There are now no remains of Wakefield Green, all of it has been enclosed, and several portions of it are built upon; and it is worthy of notice, that on the one side of the spot, where the green is said to

have been, the ground descends from Sandal to the present turnpike road, and on a tract of level ground close to Porto Bello House; and that, at a little distance further on the turnpike road leading towards Wakefield, there is a slight elevation in the road, and in the contiguous fields. After carefully viewing the ground, I came to the conclusion that this elevation, which faces the high ground at Sandal, must be considered to have been the position of the Lancastrians; and also that the battle was fought upon the level ground between it and Sandal, extending on the one side towards Porto Bello House, and on the other to the Fall Ings, and towards Pontefract Road.

In digging the foundations of Porto Bello House, and in forming the sunk fence there, human bones, broken swords, spurs, and other relics, were discovered, which were considered fully confirmatory of that locality having been the scene of the conflict. On the northern part of Fall Ings, near the side where the highway to Pontefract runs, fragments of armour, and other indications, apparently of the battle, are said to have been discovered some time ago, in making an excavation there. It was also the spot, and on the side of Sandal, where the battle would naturally take place, after the advance of the Lancastrians from York [Pontefract] to Wakefield; and it tallies with the accounts handed down to us, that the battle was fought between Wakefield and Sandal, and upon Wakefield Green.[3]

The first Ordnance Survey map of the area, produced at around the time of Brooke's visit, shows clearly the contours he mentioned. From his words we can, therefore, draw several conclusions. Firstly, that the battle was fought between four points: the castle; the site of Portobello House (*see* point 1 on Figure C); the area in Wakefield known as the 'Fall Ings' (*see* point 2 on Figure C); and the location that Burne recounts as being east of the Barnsley–Wakefield road (*see* point 3 on Figure C).

This would mean that the Lancastrians took up a starting position north of Sandal Castle, with their right flank anchored slightly forwards of a point which in modern terms could best be described as being between the bus station on the A61 and the junction with Portobello Road. This would have meant that the Lancastrians' right flank would have been anchored on the River Calder with the river acting as protection to the flank (a tactic which the Lancastrians would adopt three months later at Towton). Their left flank extended a little beyond the location of Belle Vue House. The site of this house can today be found in the middle of the grounds of the cemetery, south of the River Calder, adjacent to the A638 Wakefield–Doncaster road, and can be accessed via Sugar Lane.

A map of the area shows that this proposed Lancastrian front would have cut across what is today Bromley Mount and on through the centre of Welbeck Street and Sugar Lane, and then into the cemetery. Indeed, if one were to walk along Sugar Lane to the high point in the road about halfway along the length of the cemetery, where the ground slopes away to the south, an impressive and clear view of Sandal Castle can be obtained above the houses and trees. In my opinion, this view, even in this 'developed' age, clearly demonstrates that the high point to

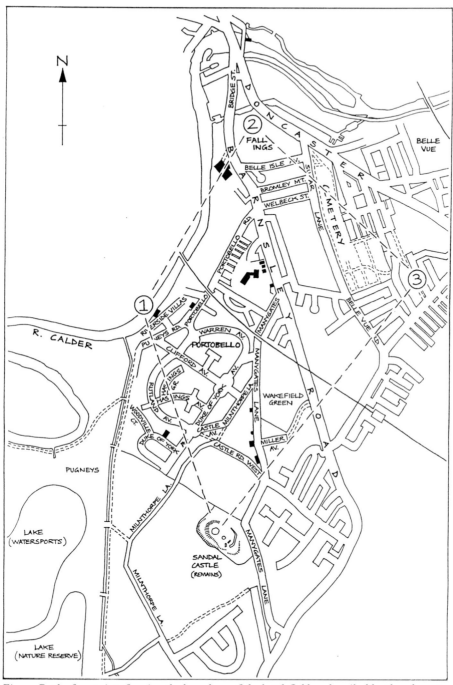

Figure C: the four points forming the boundary of the battlefield as described by the advocates of School B.

Sugar Lane. A view of Sandal Castle from the high ground upon which the Lancastrian forces mustered before the battle, to the south of Wakefield Bridge, as described by the advocates of School B. This is the same view that Brooke was able to enjoy in the 1850s, before the site was 'developed'. This view, in my opinion, clearly demonstrates that the battle was fought between this point and the castle, or as a number of chroniclers described it, 'In the plain ground between his castle and the town of Wakefield . . .'. (Author's collection)

the south of the river must have been the location of the Lancastrian front. From this vantage point they would have been able to watch the castle and its inhabitants, making this an obvious choice for a command post. Moreover, the line described above is on a direct and parallel alignment to that which Yorkist troops would have assumed as they issued out of the castle, heading for Wakefield via the bridge.

This location also fits with the words of the chroniclers, who claim that the battle was fought 'in the plain ground between his castle and the town of Wakefield'. In my opinion they are actually referring to the plain ground to the north (*see* Appendix I), not the north-west, which is more in keeping with the phrase the 'town of Wakefield'. This view is shared by many others, including Ramsay (p. 237, although he errs in supposing that the Yorkists marched out of the south-facing castle gates when the castle gates in fact face north); Tyas (p. 53); Stansfield (pp. 28–9); Markham (p. 113, although he makes the same error as Ramsay); and Barrett (p. 135).

Again, by viewing the 1850s Ordnance Survey map, we can see that the area between the castle and Wakefield is devoid of any buildings, neatly fitting the chroniclers' description of 'plain ground'.

This location places the remains found at Portobello House slightly forward of the right flank of the Lancastrian front, but this appears to fit with other clues which will be covered in subsequent chapters. Doubtless in the 1460s Sandal Castle was a formidable fortress which dominated the surrounding countryside, known then as Sandal Common (although in later years remnants of it were to become known as Wakefield Green). At that time there was a settlement called Wakefield to the north of the castle, by the River Calder, although its size is not recorded. To the east of the castle was the village and church of Sandal (known then as Sandal Magna), which probably developed there under the protection afforded by the castle. To both east and west of the castle there were vast tracts of woodland.[4]

CHAPTER FIVE

The Battle of Wakefield – 30 December 1460

Their great number shall not appal my spirits . . .

In order to recount the battle of Wakefield accurately and objectively, we shall view it from two different perspectives. In order to differentiate between these two, we shall call one the accepted account (that is, what is generally agreed to have occurred), and the other, the suggested account, an alternative which I believe represents the correct sequence of events. The majority of Victorian and modern-day historians follow – to a greater or lesser degree – the 'accepted' account; although there are a few variations in details, they all subscribe to one general scenario.

For each account, I shall offer evidence both contemporary, near contemporary, and modern, to support each theory, and allow the reader to decide which account reflects best what might have happened.

THE ACCEPTED ACCOUNT

When the Duke of York reached Sandal Castle between 21 and 24 December, he found it ill-prepared to sustain the large army which he had brought with him from southern England. The reason for this is not recorded, but one can assume that with a large Lancastrian force only a short distance away at Pontefract, the Yorkist constable of Sandal Castle was unable (or perhaps unwilling) to travel around the manor, gathering food and supplies ready for the arrival of his lord. It may be that because the Duke of York changed his plans so late in the campaign, the constable was not given sufficient warning – or even notified at all – of the Duke's intention to come to Sandal.

Whatever the reason for the poor preparations at Sandal, it still remains unlikely that the troops under the Duke's command took up residence in the castle itself. Although the strength of the castle walls and its formidable presence cannot be doubted, yet it was a relatively small castle by comparison to those at Dunstanburgh, Ludlow or Pontefract for example. It is difficult to conceive that it could accommodate within its walls an army of 500 or 600 men, never mind the

5,000 or 6,000 that the Duke of York is known to have brought with him to Sandal. (Indeed, 200 years later, during the English Civil War, the castle garrison consisted of only 100 men, and this force held out against the besieging Parliamentarian force for a considerable length of time. In fact, the castle was never taken by force of arms and was only surrendered to Parliament after the garrison agreed favourable terms.)[1]

With this being the case, it is likely that the Duke's men bivouacked in the nearby fields and wooded areas that surrounded the castle at that time. Many probably camped in and around Wakefield itself, an opinion voiced not only by some of the chroniclers, notably Davies (p. 106) and Vergil (p. 108) but also in several more recent accounts, particularly the Victorian historian Crowther (pp. 18–19), and the modern Gillingham (p. 119).

What effect this had on the local people is not recorded. However, with food in short supply and the harsh winter weather making living conditions even more difficult to bear than usual, it is likely that the Yorkist commanders encouraged their men to set out on extended foraging duties to provide victuals for the army. It is also probable that the Lancastrians at Pontefract Castle were well aware that the Duke of York was heading north, especially since the encounter at Worksop. Equally, knowing that Sandal was the Duke's principal stronghold in Yorkshire, they would certainly have had it under constant surveillance or, at the very least, on the list of places to be checked on a regular basis by their many scouts and spies.

It has been suggested that one of these foraging parties approached too near to Pontefract, thus bringing the presence of the Duke to the attention of the Lancastrians and spurring them into action. This view is mentioned in the work of Leadman (p. 354) and Freeman (p. 282).

This view, however, I feel can be discounted, simply because the Lancastrians were, in the first instance, already aware of the Yorkist movements, and secondly, they would certainly have been informed of the Duke's arrival at Sandal by their many spies and scouts. Barrett in his work (p. 133) supports my reasoning.

Aware that the Duke of York was near at hand, the Lancastrians spent the next three days (25–27 December) gathering their forces. The reason for the delay was probably that the Lancastrians also had foraging parties out around the shire gathering provisions and it would have taken some time for the commanders to muster their men. Whatever, on the morning of 28 December the Lancastrians set off towards Sandal to confront the Duke of York.

Meanwhile at Sandal, York also set about gathering his forces. The chronicler Stow commented that:

> The Duke came to the castle of Sandal besides Wakefield on Christmas Eve, and there began to assemble his tenants and friends. There came to him under the colour of friendship, the Lord Neville, brother of the Earl of Westmorland, and requested of him a commission for him to raise the people.[2]

The author of *An English Chronicle of the reigns of Richard II, Henry IV, V, VI*, wrote:

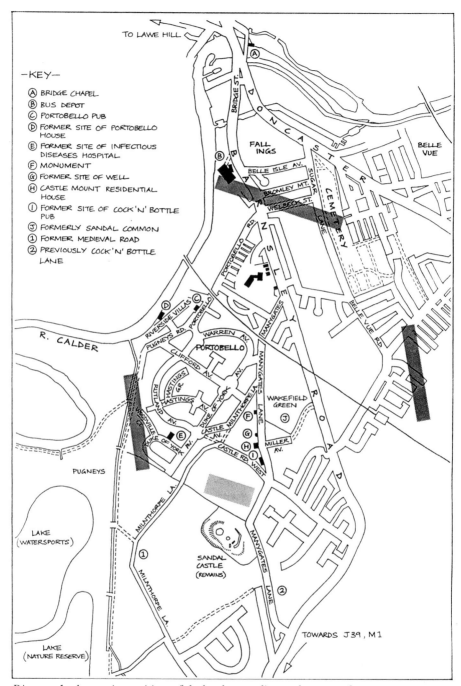

Diagram 1: the opening positions of the battle according to the accepted account.

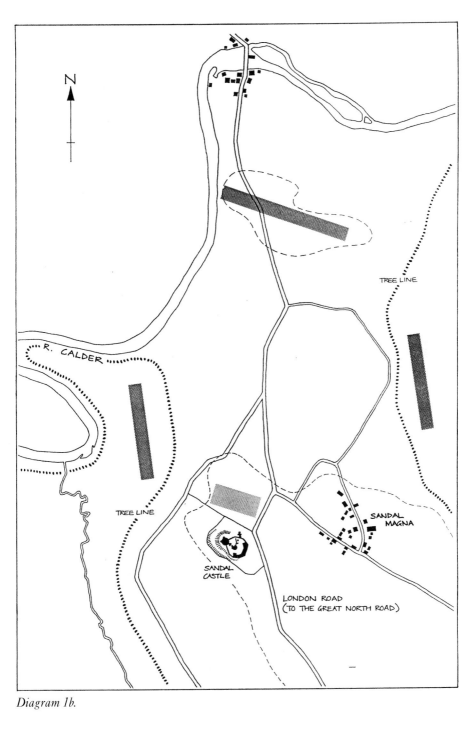

Diagram 1b.

Excavated remains of the motte and barbican of Sandal Castle. (G. Wheeler)

Then the Lord Neville, brother to the Earl of Westmorland, under false colour went to the said Duke of York, desiring a commission of him for to raise a people for to chastise the rebels of the county; and the Duke it granted.[3]

Because of the rather lengthy process of recruiting in the fifteenth century, it is, in my opinion, debatable whether the Lord Neville came to the Duke on his arrival at Sandal to ask for this commission. With the battle only three or four days hence, it is unlikely that he could have raised an army of 8,000 men in such a short space of time. It is more likely, therefore, that he sought and obtained his commission some time earlier, reporting back regularly on his progress to the Duke; once York arrived at Sandal, Neville would have come to inform him in person about his progress in recruiting.

However, the Lancastrians advanced from Pontefract towards the Yorkists at Sandal, a distance of some 9 miles. Richard Knowles, whose recent work on the battle, *The Battle of Wakefield* (1993), contains much about the topography of the battlefield, suggests that the Lancastrians travelled along the high ground through the village of Croften, close to Walton village, and then as they drew nearer to Sandal, travelled along the base of the ridge on which Walton village stands, thus being reasonably well concealed from the view of the castle look-outs.

The Lancastrian order of battle was stated by Clements Markham to have been as follows:

> Lord Clifford, with his Yorkshire friends ('the Flower of Craven'), led the van, so as to become the right wing in forming the battle, resting on the River Calder. The Dukes of Somerset and Exeter and Earls of Devon and Northumberland were in the centre. The rear, which would form the left wing in wheeling into line, was under the command of the Earl of Wiltshire.[4] Sir Andrew Trollope[5] was the principal military adviser and chief of staff.[6]

Although Markham does not give his source for this information, Edward Hall in his account gives some clues as to the Lancastrian commanders' disposition:

> The Duke of Somerset and others of the queen's part, knowing perfectly that if the Duke got the victory, their days were finished, and their livings left bare, like men quickened and exasperate, for the safeguard of their lives and defence of their goods, determined to abide the chance, and to espy their most advantage, and so appointed the Lord Clifford, to lie in the one stole (ambush), and the Earl of Wiltshire in the other, and they themselves kept the main battle.[7]

The arrival of the Lancastrian army before Sandal Castle, some time on 28 December, caused the Yorkists to retreat towards the safety afforded by Sandal Castle itself. However, unlike latter-day historians such as Ross (p. 119) and Gillingham (p. 50), who state that the whole army withdrew within the walls of the castle, it is my opinion, based on the fact that the castle could not contain so many men, that those Yorkists who were not away on foraging duties were informed of the Lancastrian approach, and took up a position outside the castle, probably on the flat ground to the north of the fortress, at the southern edge of Wakefield Green.

At this point, it appears that the centre of the Lancastrian army, led by Somerset, Northumberland and the others mentioned above, took up a position north of Wakefield Green, but south of the river, facing the Yorkists within and around the castle. The van and the rear are said to have remained concealed within the wooded areas, unseen by the Yorkists who had gathered at the castle (*see* Diagram 1).

However, no one, neither chroniclers nor modern historians, can account for how the Lancastrian van was able to manoeuvre itself to the west of Sandal Castle undetected by the Yorkists lined up to the south of Wakefield Green. With the troops from both sides in position, we are told that for the next 24 hours the Lancastrians taunted the Duke of York, trying to draw him from his stronghold. The Lancastrians, lacking siege weapons (and without the experienced personnel required to maintain the extensive building works, trenches and so on required to impose a siege) were aware that the longer the Duke of York maintained his position within the castle, then the greater the likelihood that he would be reinforced, and therefore they were desperate to draw him into battle.

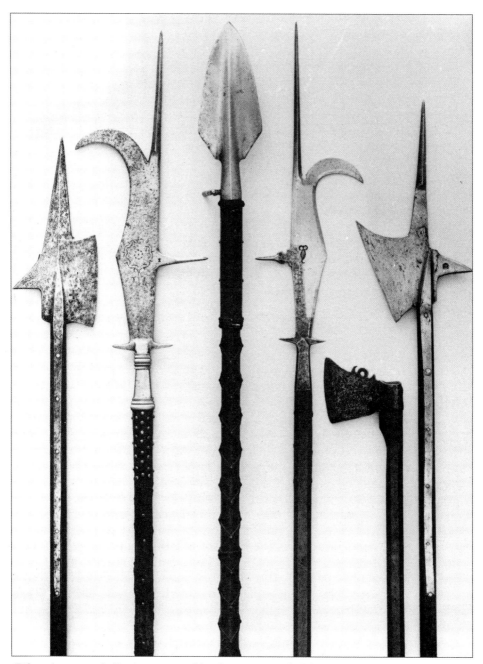

Fifteenth-century halberds, spears and battle axes, typical of those used during the battles of the Wars of the Roses. (Wallace Collection, London)

What form these taunts took is not recorded. However, they probably accused the Duke of cowardice, that he was hiding behind the walls of the castle, too scared to come out and face a woman. The issue of York being taunted by Queen Margaret is mentioned not only in the work of Freeman (p. 282) and Crowther (p. 19), but also, less reliably, in the graphic account by Stansfield (pp. 29–30). It is not supported by any of the chroniclers and the current view is that it probably did not happen. Ramsay, in contrast, says that it was the Lancastrians' 'bold advance' to Wakefield which brought the Duke of York out from behind the safety of the castle walls. Although it is clear to us that the queen was not present at Wakefield at this time, there is no reason to believe that the Duke of York was aware of that fact. Indeed, as far as he was concerned, he probably thought she was. We can never now be sure of what knowledge the Duke had about who was present in the Lancastrian ranks.

However, the taunts seem to have worked, gnawing away at the Duke of York's sense of honour, for he was keen to oblige the Lancastrians and issue forth and offer battle. It is mentioned by more than one chronicler that a meeting was held in one of the great chambers at Sandal Castle to discuss whether they should fight or wait; it is said that present at this meeting were the Duke of York, his son Edmund, Earl of Rutland, the Earl of Salisbury, Sir David Hall, and several other Yorkist commanders. Not only is this mentioned by the chronicler Hall, but it is also to be found in the pages of more modern-day historians: Tyas (p. 49), for example, also refers to the meeting.

Only Hall tells us what transpired at this meeting, but his account puts words into the mouths of the participants and should be read with caution, as it is unlikely to be an accurate representation of what was said:

> . . . and although Sir Davy Hall, his old servant and chief counseillor, advised him to keep his castle and to defend the same with his small number till his son the Earl of March were come with his power of Marchmen and Welsh soldiers; yet he would not be counselled, but in a great fury said, 'Ah, Davy, Davy, hast thou loved me so long, and now would'st have me dishonoured? Thou never saw me keep fortress when I was Regent of Normandy, when the Dauphin himself, with his puissance, came to besiege me, but like a man, and not like a bird included in a cage, I issued and fought with my enemies, to their loss ever (I thank God) and to my honour. If I have not kept my self within walls for fear of a great and strong prince, nor hid my face from any man living, wouldst thou that I, for dread of a scolding woman, whose weapon is only her tongue, and her nails, should incarcerate myself, and shut my gates? Then all men might of me wonder and all creatures may of me report dishonour, that a woman hath made me dastard, whom no man ever to this day could yet prove a coward: And surely my mind is rather to die with honour, than to live with shame; for of honour cometh fame, and of dishonour riseth infamy. Their great number shall not appall my spirits, but encourage them; for surely I think that I have there as many friends as enemies, which at joining, will either fly or take my part. Therefore advance my banner, in the name of God and St George, for surely I will fight with them, though I should fight alone.'

The Earl of Salisbury and others of his friends, seeing his courage, resolved themselves to his opinion, and ordered their men, and set them forth in warlike fashion.[8]

This was despite the advice of many of his followers, but as Stow chronicled:

The Duke having with him some fully 5,000 Men contrary to the mind of his faithful friends would needs issue forth to fight with his enemies.[9]

Thus, it appears that the Duke, viewing the Lancastrian numbers from the castle – and unaware of the concealed Lancastrian forces in the woods to either side of Sandal Castle – perceived that the Lancastrians were not as numerous as he had first been told and so issued forth to give battle. However, before he could leave the castle it appears that one of the many Yorkist foraging parties chose that moment to return to the castle, and in trying to fight their way back to the safety of the castle, became embroiled in combat with the Lancastrians to the north of Wakefield Green.

Leadman reports this as follows:

Vexed at want of success on the part of his foragers, and hunger staring him in the face, York decided to give battle to the pursuers. This step was taken against the advice of Sir David Hall, who strongly urged him to await help from the Earl of March.[10]

Wakefield Green looking south-east. It was on and around this area that the final stages of the battle of Wakefield were fought. (Author's collection)

With this, the Duke 'trusting to his owne knowledge in warefare' as Polydore Vergil put it, sallied forth from the castle down onto Wakefield Green, towards the waiting Lancastrians. This initial move is well chronicled:

> . . . trusting to his owne knowledge in warfare, and the valience of his soldiers, yssued out of his campe against his enemyes in good array.[11]

Edward Hall's account is rather more vocal:

> The Duke of York with his people, descended down the hill in good order and array and was suffered to pass forward, toward the main battle: but when he was in the plain ground between his castle and the town of Wakefield . . .[12]

Stow's report was very similar:

> The Duke of York with his people descended down the hill in good order of array, and had suffered to pass on toward the main battle: but when he was in the plain field between his castle and the town of Wakefield . . . [13]

These accounts, although similar, also give a good indication of where the battle took place, 'in the plain field between his castle and the town of Wakefield', or, as it is known today, Wakefield Green. Thus the two sides joined in battle. Unfortunately, there is no indication of the time when the battle began, although in my opinion it was probably early in the afternoon, between midday and 2 o'clock.

Many of the Duke's men would have been mounted, and as they issued forth from the castle and charged towards the enemy, the Lancastrians, still harassing York's foraging party as it tried to fight its way to the castle, also began to advance. The Yorkists no doubt sallied forth under the banners of the Duke of York, bearing the usual device of the Plantagenet family; the Duke's own banner was a falcon volant argent, within a fetterlock. In this battle, however, the banner had changed slightly, the falcon having its wing extended as if trying to open the lock, in reference it is said (by the historian Markham) to York's claim to the throne, the throne being represented by the lock itself.

The Yorkists charged deep into the fray, withstanding an arrow storm let loose by the Lancastrians as they traversed the ground between them. It is likely that the two sides came to blows in a line running east from the site of Portobello House, thus explaining why remains from the battle were found there many years later (*see* Diagram 2).

It was customary during the battles of this period for the opposing sides to line up facing each other for some time before hostilities began, thus allowing the heralds the opportunity to seek a peaceful solution. It appears that no such pause occurred at Wakefield. The armies would generally muster themselves into three groups or battles: the vanguard (or van), which usually made up the right flank, the centre (or middle), and the rearguard (or rear), which usually made up the left flank of a battle formation.[14]

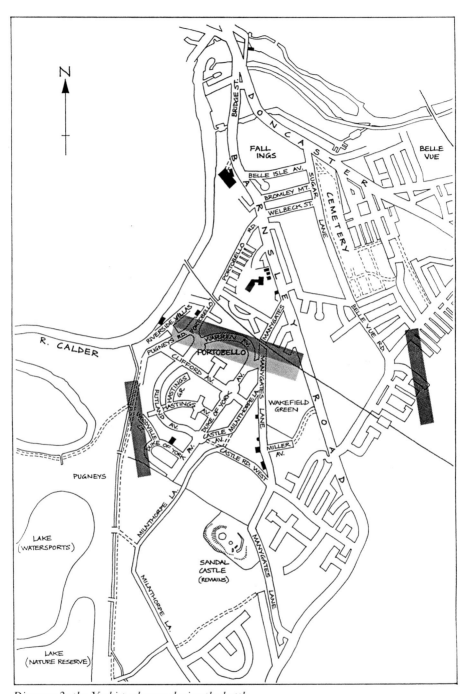

Diagram 2: the Yorkist advance during the battle.

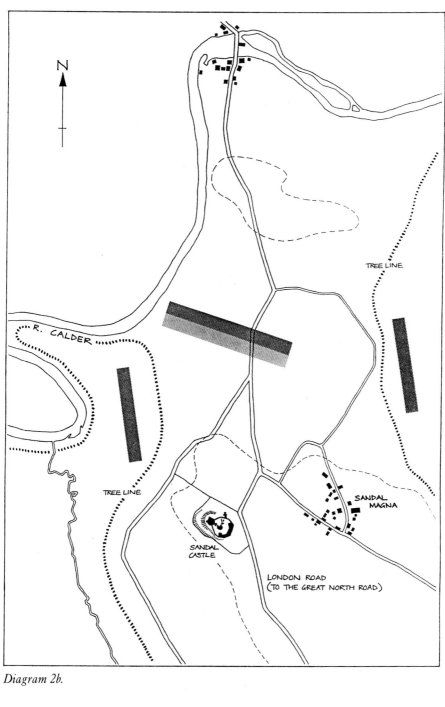

Diagram 2b.

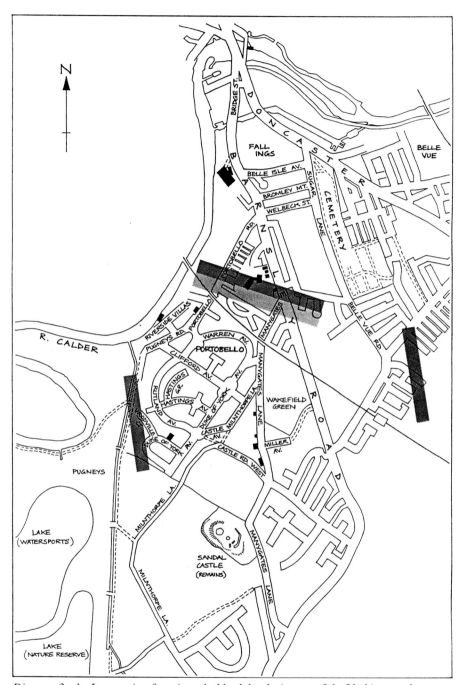

Diagram 3: the Lancastrian front is pushed back by the impact of the Yorkist attack.

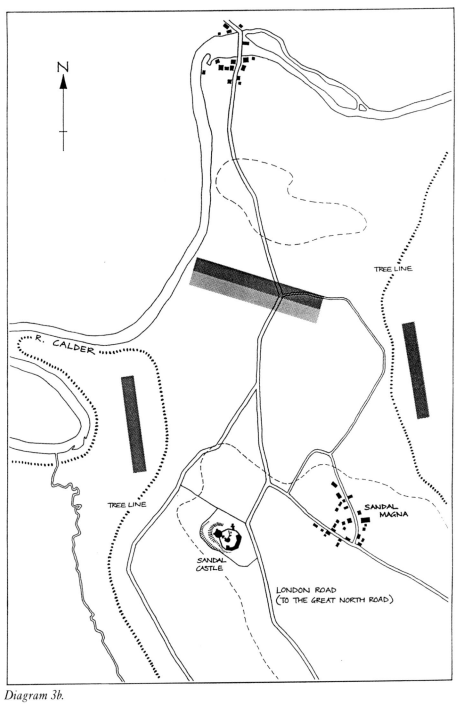

Diagram 3b.

Generally, after squaring up to each other, the start of the conflict was usually signalled by an exchange of archery fire. The archers, the elite of most armies, would stand a little forward of the main army in order to facilitate the first salvo. After both sides had fired their arrows, the two sides would advance towards each other, with the archers melting into the rest of the troops, who were predominantly billmen but from the 1460s onwards handgunners as well. This was usually followed by the commencement of the mêlée. Once again, however, this was not the case at Wakefield. It is said that the Lancastrians were short of archers, and that as the Yorkists charged from the castle directly at them, the usual preambles were ignored at this battle and the two sides plunged straight in to the deadly mêlée.

Unwittingly, of course, the Duke had been drawn into a trap. Unaware that there were Lancastrians concealed within the woods on either side, he charged deep into the ranks of the enemy, coming to the support of the survivors of the foraging party, and pushing the Lancastrian front back towards the River Calder (*see* Diagram 3). If we accept this account then it supports the argument that at the start of the battle the Lancastrians would have been situated a little to the south of what is known today as the 'Fall Ings', an area which, as Brooke described, was given that name because of the large numbers of combatants who fell there in this battle.

It appears that the Yorkists, many of whom were mounted, came off the better in the first assault, while the Lancastrians, most of whom were on foot, reeled under the initial shock of the impact, and were forced to give ground, pushed back upon the route along which they had advanced. Whether this 'giving up of ground' was a deliberate ploy by the Lancastrians to draw the Yorkists further away from the sanctuary of the castle is unknown. All we know for certain is that shortly after this the trap was sprung, and the concealed Lancastrians issued forth from the woods and attacked the Yorkists on both flanks and from the rear (*see* Diagram 4).

These opening moves and the subsequent encircling manoeuvre is well documented by the chroniclers. Polydore Vergil wrote:

> At the beginning the fight was mightily mainteyned mutually, while that a great part of them who were in the front battaile being killed, the Duke of Yorkes small number was environed of the multitude.[15]

And Hall the following:

> . . . but when he was in the plain ground between his castle and the town of Wakefield, he was environed [surrounded] on every side, like a fish in a net, or a deer in a buck-stall . . .[16]

Stow wrote:

> . . . but when he was in the plain field between his castle and the town of Wakefield, he was environed on every side . . .[17]

The troops employed to carry out these flanking attacks were lightly armoured infantry or light cavalry (often known as 'prickers' after the 15-ft lances they carried, which were used to discourage deserters from leaving the ranks whilst on the march during campaigns). Light troops could obviously cover the distance from the woods to the mêlée much more quickly. It cannot, however, be proved whether it was a dual flanking attack or whether the attack came from just one side. In either case, the result was deadly.

The Yorkists, surrounded on every side, had no choice but to fight for their lives. It is not unreasonable to assume that when they realised that they had been trapped and now faced overwhelming odds they attempted a fighting retreat towards the castle, so that the battle flowed back along the Wakefield–Sandal road (later known as Cock and Bottle Lane) They might have made it too, had fate not then dealt a deadly blow to the beleaguered Duke of York – treachery.

Lord Neville took the field at that point with some 8,000 troops, originally commissioned to come to the Duke of York's aid; but Neville declared for the Lancastrians and his act sealed the fate of the Yorkist army. His change of sides was noted by the author of *An English Chronicle of the reigns of Richard II, Henry IV, V, VI*, who wrote:

> Then the Lord Neville, brother to the Earl of Westmorland, under false colour . . . raised a number of 8,000 men, and brought them to the lords of the country; that is to say, the Earl of Northumberland, Lord Clifford, and Duke of Somerset, that were adversaries and enemies to Duke Richard.[18]

There was to be no escape; all that was left was to die bravely. Stansfield's account of the battle takes up the story:

> The engagement now became wider and fiercer, and the carnage was frightful. If the Lancastrians were weak in archers, they were strong in swordsmen, who now wielded their arms with deadly effect at such close quarters. The duke's handful of troops fought with surpassing courage against the vastly superior forces of the enemy, and for a time the fortunes of the day wavered in the balance . . .
> . . . the battle soon began to assume an unfavourable aspect for the Yorkists. Still the brave army of Richard fought on gallantly against overpowering odds. Wherever his presence was most needed, there was Richard in the thickest of the fight, animating his men by his dauntless bearing, and urging them on by his ringing war cry. His matchless valour was conspicuous on all sides, and he inspired his followers with a spirit of indomitable bravery almost equal to his own.
> The uproar of the battle swelled mightier and mightier; the shock of steed, the clash of steel, the hiss of arrows, the shouts of the victors, and the cries of the wounded, all told that the crisis of the battle was come. Father fought against son, brother against brother, and kith against kin; and the fight was so deadly, very little quarter was given on either side. More cavalry and infantry arrived on the scene, fresh and panting for the fray, and shouting 'Exeter to the onslaught!'[19]

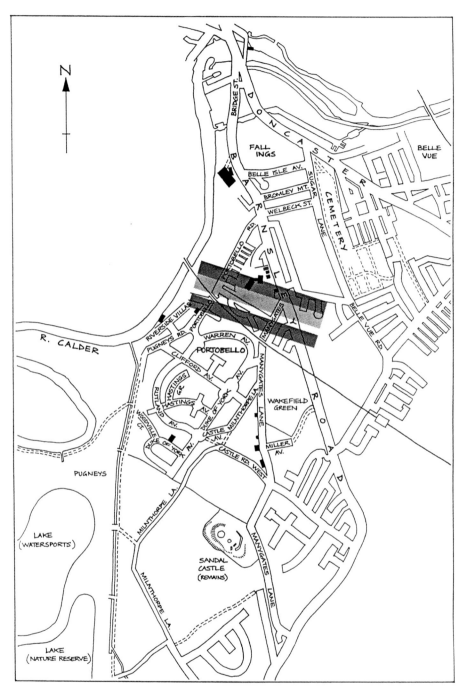

Diagram 4: the Lancastrians encircle the Yorkists 'like a fish in a net or a deer in a buck-stall'.

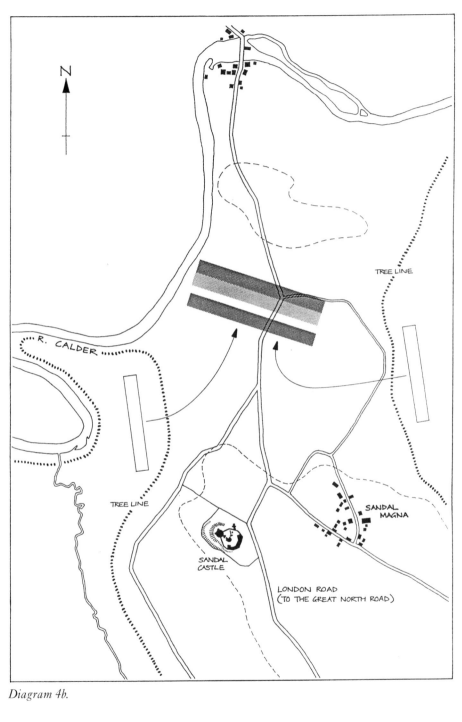

Diagram 4b.

Manygates Lane looking north towards Wakefield Green, from a point a little beyond where the Cock and Bottle public house once stood. This lane was previously called Cock and Bottle Lane.

> . . . though his warrior yeoman were thrown into disorder, still the untiring might of Richard's arm defied for a time the wave upon wave of troops that attacked his doomed army; but as well attempt to stem the tide of ocean as for that scattered army to resist the overwhelming torrent of foes that rushed upon them . . .[20]

Although this account of the battle is greatly romanticized, I have included it because I feel it captures not only the spirit of the Duke of York, but also the atmosphere of the battlefield.

Towards the end, the Duke of York gave thought to the safety of his son, Edmund, Earl of Rutland. It is not known whether the Earl was involved in the actual battle, or viewed it from some vantage point. In either case, the Duke managed to get a message to him ordering him to flee. Perhaps the decision was made by the Earl's tutor – Sir Robert Aspall – who accompanied him. Whatever, they made the decision to leave the field.

The Duke meanwhile was killed on the field of battle, although the circumstances of his death are unknown. He is said to have died fighting, facing his enemies and with his back to a clump of three willow trees (for protection). Markham gives the following account:

Drawing of the large gold ring found on the battlefield near to the place where the Duke of York died. The motto reads, 'por bon amour', which translates as 'in true love', or 'in good love'. Reproduced from Walker's History of Wakefield. *(G. Wheeler)*

The Duke of York fell fighting to the last. Camden says that there was a small space, hedged round, enclosing a stone cross on the spot where the Duke fell; and Gibson adds that there, before the civil war between Charles I and his parliament, the owners were obliged, by tenure, to keep the hedge. A very ancient willow long marked the spot but it has been cut down within the last few years.[21] On the spot where the Duke and his faithful friends made their last stand an antique ring was found. Within it was engraved the words *Por bon amour* (meaning either 'for good love' or 'in true love') and on one side was wrought the effigies of the Virgin Mary, our saviour, and two other saints. The ring formed part of Thoresby's [exhibition at the] Museum[22] at Leeds.[23]

On the issue of the location of the Duke's last stand, Tyas, writing in 1854, made reference to Mr Norisson Scatcherd, who remarked:

This spot on the right [travelling in the direction of Sandal from Wakefield] of the lane or the old road leading from Wakefield to the Three Houses [a public house] in Sandal, and which was once the London road, is a triangular piece of ground, with a fence about it, which the tenant of the place is bound, by his lease, to maintain. When I saw it, many years ago, some very old trees were growing in the fence, and vestiges of others, still older, were perceptible . . .[24]

In pinpointing this spot, Brooke, who visited and described the battlefield in 1852, mentions the site of the duke's demise as follows:

On the right hand side of the road leading from Wakefield to Barnsley, which passes the castle, and is called Sandal Castle Lane [previously Cock and Bottle Lane and today (1996) Manygates Lane], is a small field or close, or rather a triangle form, which is said to be the spot where the Duke of York fell.

It will scarcely admit of any doubt that this is the identical place which is mentioned in the addition to Camden's *Britannia*, although there is no vestige of the cross now left. As the place is rather nearer to the castle than to the field of battle, it is not unreasonable to infer that the Duke of York may have been mortally wounded, and have been removed to a little distance in the rear (the spot in question would be in the rear of the Yorkist army), or he may have endeavoured to escape, on finding that the day was against him, and may have been slain there in his flight. The strong probability is that it is the place where he fell. The small field or close may easily be distinguished: it lies about a mile from Wakefield Bridge, and at a very trifling distance beyond the toll-bar, a little well will be remarked,[25] in the hedge, on the right side of the old road to Barnsley; and about midway between the toll-bar and the well, the small field or close presents itself to view.

It is remarkable for having two very old willows growing in the hedge adjoining the road; and more of them were not very long ago growing there. A small compartment of the field was, within the recollection of the recent vicar of Sandal, fenced off from the remainder of it, and planted with red and white roses, which must naturally be supposed to have been done to commemorate the battle, or the death of the Duke of York.[26]

The actual circumstances of York's death are not recorded, although the tradition of his 'last stand', with his back to a clump of willow trees, seems to have survived the test of time. It is prominent not only in the works of Stansfield (p. 40) but also in the works of Crowther (p. 20). Some historians say that he refused quarter, preferring death before such dishonour. Stanfield picked up on this point in his own account as follows:

At the foot of the steep road which winds from the castle to the lower ground stood at that time some huge trees, and it was with his back to these trees that Richard, with his decimated ranks of gallant soldiers, made his last stand. His rear protected by these gigantic trunks, his front entrenched behind the heaps of the slain, for round this spot had waged the brunt of the battle and the deadliest of the fight, Richard had never before in all his former wars surpassed himself as in this, his last fight; and here, with irresistible valour and with sublime despair, he still fought on.

The fury of the conflict and the pressure of the excited rear ranks impelled the Lancastrians on, and at length Richard's followers were forced back, and he himself was unhorsed, wounded and beaten to his knees. Many wished to spare him, and were reluctant to strike, but yield he would not! Amidst the din of battle and the victorious cries of the victors were heard loud shouts of 'Yield!, yield thee!'.[27] Some of Richard's brave soldiers strove to cover his body, but numbers rushed on and swept the gallant defenders away, and a hundred blows

A modern day representation of the Duke of York's 'last stand' by Graham Shaw. The story of his last stand, with his back to three willow trees, appears to have stood the test of time, despite not being mentioned in any contemporary chronicle. (Author's collection)

rained down on the Duke's armour, and he at last fell, still grasping his sword in his iron hand.[28]

All we can say for certain is that York's death, in sight of his ancestral home, brought about the end of the battle and the beginning of the Yorkist rout. In total, in addition to the majority of the Yorkist commanders present, there were slain some 2,000 to 2,500 Yorkist troops (*see* Appendix III).

The duration of the battle is not certain, with the various chroniclers again not agreeing, but it was probably less than an hour. Hall's account stated that Richard was 'within half an hour slain and dead, and his whole army discomforted',[29] and

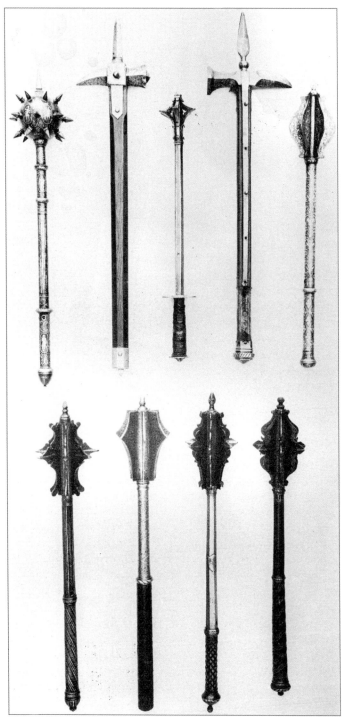

War hammers and maces typical of the types used during the battles of the Wars of the Roses. (Wallace Collection, London)

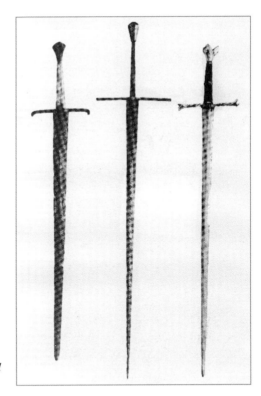

Sixteenth-century swords in the Tower of London; the two on the left are English and the one on the right is German.

Stow records that, 'so that he manfully fighting was within half hour slain, and his whole army discomforted and with him died of his true friends'.[30] In contrast, Polydore Vergil claims that Margaret's force 'vanquished the residue of her enemyes in the moment of one houre'.[31] My own view is that the battle lasted somewhere in the region of an hour, while the subsequent pursuit of the Yorkists in the rout may have lasted well into the evening, and certainly for several hours. In most battles the heaviest casualties occur when one side breaks and retreats, and there is no reason to believe that this was not the case at Wakefield. One could perhaps argue that since the Yorkists were surrounded, then this battle may be the exception, because the rout of a surrounded force would surely differ from that of an army fighting on a single front.

However, assuming that a typical rout occurred, then significant numbers of Yorkists may have tried to reach sanctuary by fleeing towards the town of Wakefield. Many of the Yorkists, hotly pursued by the Lancastrians, would have been killed before actually crossing the river. This may explain how that area of Wakefield acquired then the name it still retains today, 'Fall Ings'. If this is correct, then it would also explain the presence there of Lord Clifford and his men, when their battle had been fought further south. (His actions there are covered in a subsequent chapter.)

The final action from the conflict to be mentioned here is alleged to have occurred early in the mêlée, and is mentioned by Stansfield (p. 43) in his account of the battle:

> The castle having been left entirely unguarded was taken early in the day by a party belonging to Lord Wiltshire's force . . .[32]

Disregarding for the moment the debate over the Earl of Wiltshire's presence on the field (*see* Appendix III), it is clear that at some point the castle was indeed occupied by the Lancastrians. Although it is unlikely that it was taken 'early in the day', it is difficult to pinpoint when it happened. I think it is fair to suggest that the Lancastrian capture of the castle was achieved only after the Yorkists had been defeated. It is likely that any Yorkists remaining in the castle would have been watching the battle from the vantage point afforded by the castle walls, and would soon have realized that the day was lost. Watching the slaughter, and aware that if captured they would probably suffer the same fate, they probably took the opportunity to leave the fortress – and the vicinity – before the Lancastrians had time to turn their thoughts to occupying the castle.

THE SUGGESTED ACCOUNT

So we come to the second version of what happened at the battle of Wakefield. There is little argument that the Duke of York arrived at Sandal to find the castle ill-prepared to sustain his forces, and that consequently the Yorkist commanders instructed many of their men to travel the shire in search of victuals. Most people further agree that the Lancastrians were alerted – either by scouts reporting the Duke's movements or as a result of one of these foraging parties straying too close to Pontefract – to the Yorkists' arrival at Sandal. It seems reasonable to say that the Lancastrians arrived at Sandal some time on 28 December, or at the very least were in position – at Sandal – before the morning of the 29th. So this account begins with both sides encamped within and before the castle.

The lack of supplies was a constant worry to the Yorkist commanders. The presence of the Lancastrians was unlikely to have prevented (although it certainly hindered) the Yorkists from despatching their men around the shire in search of supplies. Indeed, William of Worcester's account of the battle says that foraging parties were still leaving Sandal Castle on 29 December: 'The followers of the Duke of York, having gone out to forage for provisions on the 29th of December'.[33] Therefore, we can conclude that there were a number of foraging parties – not just the ones which left the castle on 29 December – that had not yet returned to the castle before the Lancastrians arrived on the 28th. Is it possible that so large a force of Lancastrians could remain 'concealed' in the surrounding countryside, without being noticed by the many foragers. This suggests that the whole of the Lancastrian army must have been encamped to the north of Wakefield Green in full view of the Yorkist army (*see* Diagram 5). If this argument is accepted, then one must ask the question, what could have provoked the Duke of York, a man whose military skill and prowess were renowned, to venture forth and attack a hostile force that he knew outnumbered his own? It has been suggested by other historians that York brought about his own death through his impulsiveness. The view that York was prone to such behaviour is reinforced by his ill-considered claim to the throne when he returned to London after the battle of Northampton. It also seems to be supported by Hall's description of the meeting that took place between York and his advisors in the great hall of Sandal Castle before the battle; and by the Bishop of Terni, who wrote that the Duke had made a 'rash advance'. (This is mentioned in the *Calendar of State Papers and Manuscripts existing in the Archives and Collections of Milan*, Vol. I, 1385–1618, ed. A.B. Hinds, p. 39, fo. 52.)

However, we should be wary of taking Hall's account at face value, as we know that he tended to write speeches for the participants when he clearly had no knowledge of what was said. In order to put this into some perspective we can draw a comparison between the events at Wakefield and the similar situation that York faced at Ludford Bridge in 1459. Although outnumbered in both instances, at Ludford, rather than risk a pitched battle he knew he could not win, York chose to flee instead – hardly the actions of a rash and impetuous commander.

In recent years much has been made of this, and many theories have been put forward. One suggests that the Duke was tricked by some of Trollope's men, who, it is said, had dressed in the livery of the Earl of Warwick's men, thus fooling York into believing that reinforcements had arrived. At this, the Duke and his followers sallied forth from the castle to strike at the Lancastrians, believing that these reinforcements would be sufficient to bring about a comfortable victory for the House of York. There is some early evidence to support this – in Jean de Waurin's chronicle we read:

. . . Andrew Trollope, who was a very subtle man of war, told the Duke of Somerset that they would not be able to get the Duke of York outside the town [castle] without consequent human losses.

They therefore prepared 400 of the most courageous men, well indoctrinated for what they had to do – i.e. they were to go into the town [castle] and tell the Duke that they were coming from Lancashire to rescue him. When the Duke of York, that never suspected such betrayal, saw all those people coming to him, he was so happy that he let them in straight away. That same night the Duke of York organised for somebody to be on the watch in order to make sure that the Duke of Somerset was in the field and observe the extent of his power.

But at the dawn of the day Andrew Trollope accompanied by other warriors, informed the Duke of York, without introducing themselves, that they were coming to rescue him, which made the Duke so joyful that he went outside the town to fight his enemies.

It was then that Andrew Trollope betrayed him, knowing the Duke of Somerset to be nearby, started the skirmish and the Duke of Somerset who was ready, charged viciously the Duke of York and his allies against whom Andrew Trollope and his troops turned swiftly and so did the people sent by him the night before to the town . . . .[34]

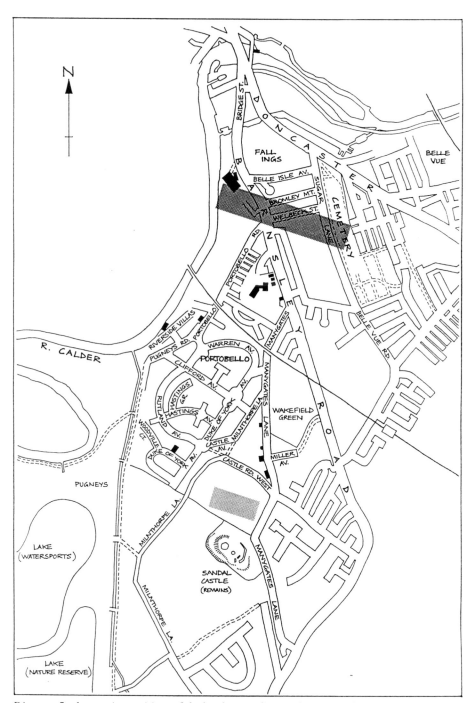

Diagram 5: the opening positions of the battle according to the suggested account.

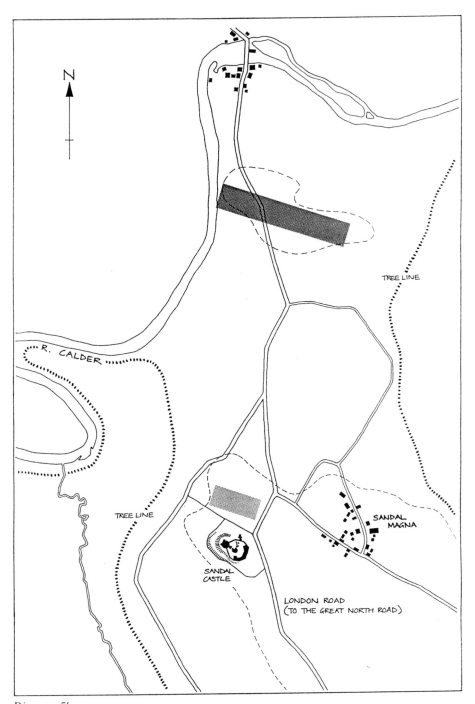

Diagram 5b.

Sallet c. *1480. (Herbert Art Gallery and Museum, Coventry)*

Since de Waurin is the only chronicler to mention this, I feel it can be discounted for several reasons. Firstly, Waurin was a close ally and friend of the Earl of Warwick, and was compiling a pro-Yorkist account of York's defeat. This point was not lost on Goodman, who wrote, in *The Wars of the Roses*: 'Waurin has a circumstantial but largely uncorroborated account of the ruses which the Lancastrian employed to undermine Yorkist defences.'[35]

It is likely that the Duke would have had word that Warwick's men were near. Sandal Castle was not under close siege, and messengers would have been able to pass back and forth with ease. Therefore, the Duke would have been able to judge Warwick's proximity to the castle – or not – before committing his men to battle. The Earl of Salisbury, plus several others from the Neville household, were inside Sandal, and would surely have been able to recognize either Warwick himself or his retainers had they been on the field.

My explanation then as to why the Duke charged out on 30 December to give battle, is as follows. We should recall that when York first arrived at the castle he set about gathering his 'tenants and friends'; in the words of John Stow:

The Duke came to the castle of Sandal besides Wakefield on Christmas Eve, and there began to assemble his tenants and friends. There came to him under the colour of friendship, the Lord Neville, brother of the Earl of Westmorland, and requested of him a commission for him to raise the people.'[36]

It was only later that the Duke was to learn that Neville had come to him 'under false colour', or as the author of *An English Chronicle of the reigns of Richard II, Henry IV, V, VI*, was to write:

> Then the Lord Neville, brother to the Earl of Westmorland, under false colour went to the said Duke of York, desiring a commission of him for to raise a people for to chastise the rebels of the county; and the Duke it granted, deeming that he had true and on his part. When he had his commission he raised a number of 8,000 men, and brought them to the lords of the country; that is to say, the Earl of Northumberland, Lord Clifford, and the Duke of Somerset, that were adversaries and enemies to Duke Richard.[37]

The crux of the argument put forward in this suggested account, is dependent on exactly when Neville showed his hand. It is my belief, that Neville did not come to the Duke at Sandal to obtain his commission, but contacted him at some point earlier – probably during York's march north to Wakefield from London. The reasoning behind this is that it would have taken more than the three or four days between York's arrival at Sandal and the alleged meeting with Neville, and the battle itself, for him to raise the 8,000 troops he is said to have brought to Wakefield.[38] Neville's status in society meant that he would not have had a standing retinue of anyway near that size. Therefore, this reference by Stow probably means that Neville, sent messages to the Duke at Sandal, rather than going in person, informing him of his progress in raising levies on the Duke's behalf.

It is generally agreed that the Yorkists committed their forces to battle in order to come to the aid of one of their foraging parties which had come under attack on its return to the fortress, on Wakefield Green to the north of Sandal Castle. However, is it likely that the Duke would have risked his entire force to save a relatively small contingent? On balance, I think it very unlikely. During the battle of Towton, three months later, the Lancastrian army held its position while Lord Clifford and the 'flower of Craven' were destroyed by a contingent of Yorkist cavalry, despite being only a relatively short distance from the Lancastrian lines, but a considerable distance from the advancing Yorkist army.[39]

If this is the case, then some other factor must have caused the Duke of York to join battle at Wakefield. Could it have been, that when the foraging party came under attack, the Lord Neville – who had still not declared his hand – came on the scene under the guise of supporting the Yorkists? If, as I believe, Lord Neville was in constant communication with the Duke, then his arrival on the field of battle would not have been unexpected. Neville's 8,000 men added to the Duke of York's 5,000 would have made the odds against the 15,000–18,000 Lancastrians much more appealing to the Duke, and might have persuaded him to leave the safety of the castle and attack the Lancastrians.

Perhaps this is what de Waurin meant when he wrote:

> . . . accompanied by other warriors, informed the Duke of York, without introducing themselves, that they were coming to rescue him, which made the Duke so joyful that he went outside the town [castle] to fight his enemies.[40]

Elizabethan portrait of John, 9th Lord Clifford (inset), and the gateway to his family home, Skipton Castle, Yorkshire. (G. Wheeler)

We should also bear in mind the words of Hall, who suggested that the Duke claimed:

> Their great number shall not appall my spirits, but encourage them; for surely I think that I have there as many friends as enemies, which at joining, will either fly or take my part. Therefore advance my banner, in the name of God and St George, for surely I will fight with them, though I should fight alone.[41]

Did the Duke still believe the Lord Neville was his friend and ally? We will never be certain of the facts of this matter, but we should remember that in the more reliable chronicle of William of Worcester, it is written that:

Garter stall plate of Richard Neville,
Earl of Salisbury, c. 1436–1460,
St George's Chapel, Windsor.
(G. Wheeler)

> . . . a dreadful battle was fought at Wakefield between the Duke of Somerset, the Earl of Northumberland and Lord Neville . . .[42]

The important words here are 'and Lord Neville', which suggests that Neville's force was independent from the main Lancastrian army. Was it these men that de Waurin was referring to? Is it possible that the men dressed in the livery of Lord Neville, were in later years chronicled as the men of Richard Neville, the Earl of Warwick? Although they were different branches of the same family, it is not unreasonable to assume that their family emblems could be confused and that out of this confusion was born the story that these men were purposely dressed in the livery of Warwick's men to trick the Duke of York into believing that reinforcements had arrived. It is, I agree, difficult to prove and is thus only put forward as a suggestion.

The issue is further complicated by the debate over Lord Neville's approach to the battle. Which direction did he come from? There are two possibilities. The first is that he advanced from the south of Sandal Castle, and manoeuvred towards the Lancastrians, along with the Duke of York's men, who joined with him when he reached the castle. On approaching the Lancastrians, the men under Neville's command turned on the Yorkists. If this was the case, it would explain

The seals of Richard Neville, Earl of Warwick 'The Kingmaker' (above) and of Richard Neville, Earl of Salisbury (below). It is possible that historians writing many years after the battle confused the followers of John Neville with those of the Earl of Warwick. (G. Wheeler)

why the Yorkists were so quickly surrounded (*see* Diagram 6). The second is that he approached the battlefield from the north, from the direction of Wakefield bridge, and his appearance may have led the Duke of York to believe that he had the opportunity to catch the Lancastrians in a pincer movement, and so he advanced from the castle (*see* Diagram 7).

My own personal view is that the second possibility is the more likely. Assuming it to be the case, then it could only have been after the Duke of York had already crossed Wakefield Green and joined the fray that he realized that Lord Neville was opposing him. Thus betrayed, the Duke and his small army of faithful followers were soon encircled by the vastly superior numbers of the Lancastrians, and their fate was sealed, as described in the 'accepted' account.

Knowles and Dockray, working together and equally drawing on contemporary accounts and using their knowledge of the topography of the battlefield, suggest that there is yet another possible solution to the conundrum of Wakefield. Their account suggests that the Duke and his army, having been drawn from the safety of the castle, and after advancing north towards the Lancastrians, were attacked in their right flank by a force which had been concealed by the ridge on which Sandal Castle stands. This attack from the east caused the Yorkist front to turn clockwise through 90 degrees, and ultimately caused their army to be pushed back towards the river, away from the castle, towards Portobello House and also towards their ultimate demise. We should not dismiss this theory out of hand as it would certainly explain why so many remnants of the battle can be found near to that spot (putting aside for the moment the suggestion of the 'natural grave pit', *see* Chapter 7). However, it does go against the arguments outlined above as to whether it would have been possible for a force of any significant size to remain concealed so near to the castle. If we accept the fact that the Yorkists had scouts and foragers travelling all over the locality, and that they were consequently already aware of the Lancastrian presence, then the probability of a surprise flank attack is diminished.

THE DATE OF THE BATTLE

Even the date of this controversial battle is open to question. Again, we must look to the evidence supplied by the chronicles. William of Worcester reported that:

> The followers of the Duke of York, having gone out to forage for provisions on the 29th of December, a dreadful battle was fought at Wakefield.[43]

This account suggests that the battle was fought on 29 December, whereas the author of *An English Chronicle of the reigns of Richard II, Henry IV, V, VI* suggested the following:

> And when they saw a convenient time for to fill yheir crul intent, the last day of December they fell upon the said Duke Richard . . .[44]

This suggests 31 December as the day the battle was fought. This is also the date given by de Waurin mentions in his chronicle:

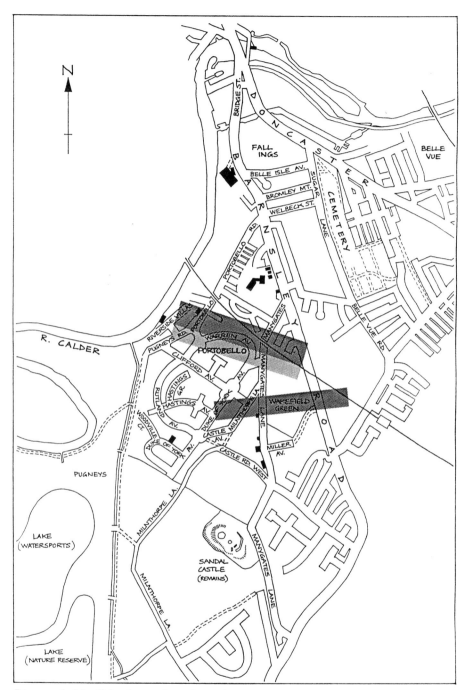

Diagram 6: Neville's advance from the south.

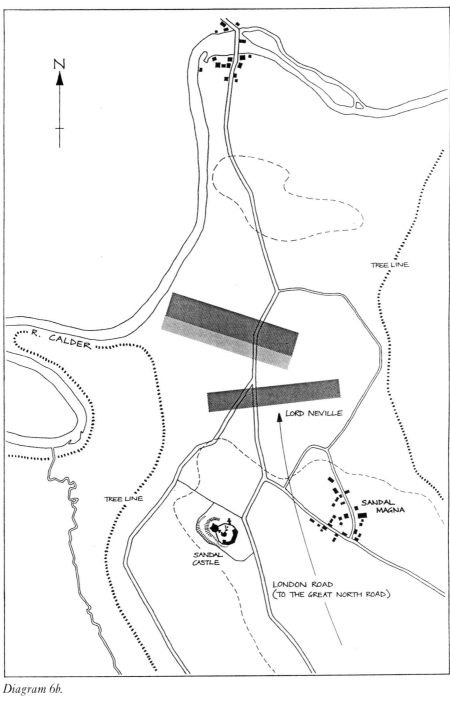

Diagram 6b.

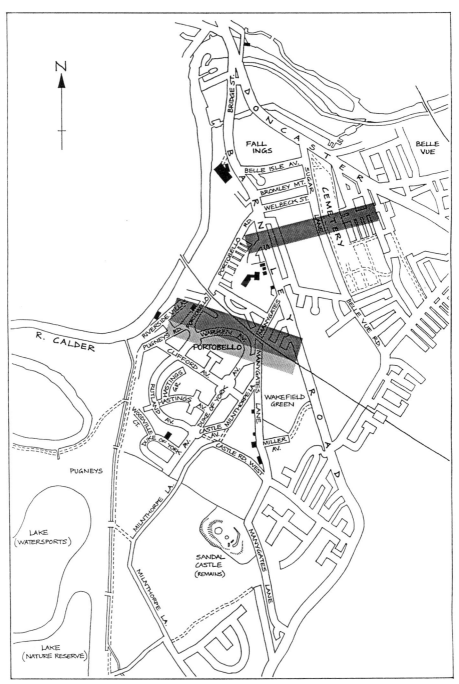

Diagram 7: Neville's advance from the north.

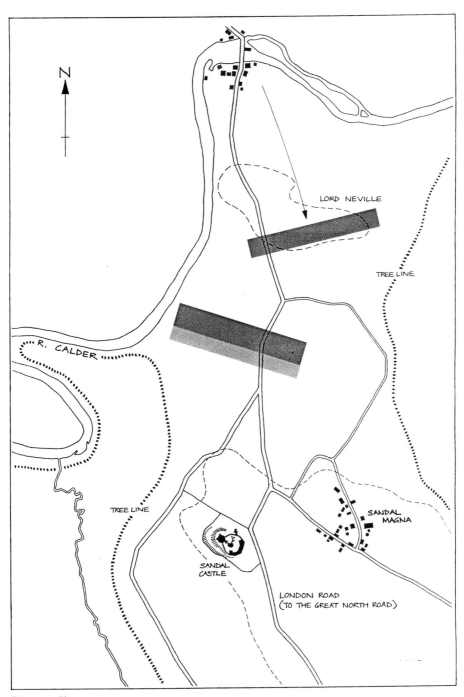

Diagram 7b.

This battle took place in front of the town of Wakefield on December 31st, 1460. Queen Margaret was very satisfied with the outcome of the battle as well as all the people supporting her cause.[45]

So, if we take the middle ground, and say that 30 December was the day the battle was fought, we cannot be far wrong, and indeed there is evidence to support this date. Not only is it mentioned in extracts from a Roman Breviary in York Minster Library, (*Test. Ebor*, vol. IV), it is also mentioned in *The Maire of Bristowe is Kalender* by Robert Ricart, town clerk of Bristol (18 Edward IV, Camden Society, 1872) as follows:

This yere [1460] the Tewisday aftir Christmas [the 30th], was slayne Richard Duke of Yorke . . .

Further, in the Act of Attainder (*see* Appendix IV) it is written:

. . . at Wakefield in the shire of York on Tywesday XXX day Decembr' last past [1460], with grete despite and cruell violence, horrible and unmanly tyrannye murdered the seid right noble Prynce Duc of York.

CHAPTER SIX

Aftermath

. . . By God's blood, thy father slew mine, and so I shall do thee . . .

THE DEATH OF THE EARL OF RUTLAND

In the 'accepted' account of the battle I discussed the rout and pursuit of the Yorkists towards Wakefield Bridge, which seems to fit well with the following events. At a point close to the end of the battle, there occurred what Brooke would later describe in his paper on the battle of Wakefield as an act of 'shocking wickedness and barbarity'. He went on:

> Edmund Plantagenet, Earl of Rutland, a son of the Duke of York, a boy only twelve years old, was captured when flying with his Tutor from the field of battle, and was put to death near Wakefield bridge, by Lord Clifford: a murder which obtained for him during the very short remainder of his life, the epithet of 'the Butcher'.[1]

Brooke was obviously working from the chronicles of Leland and Hall, where the latter describes Rutland's death as follows:

> While this battle was in fighting, a priest called Sir Robert Aspall, chaplain and schoolmaster to the young Earl of Rutland, second son to the above-named Duke of York, scarce of the age of twelve years, a fair gentleman and a maidenlike person, perceiving that flight was more safeguard than tarrying, both for him and his master, secretly conveyed the earl out of the field, by the Lord Clifford's band towards the town, but ere he could enter into a house, he was by the said Lord Clifford spied, followed, and taken, and by reason of his appearance, demanded what he was.
>
> The young gentleman, dismayed, had not a word to speak, but kneeled on his knees imploring mercy, and desiring grace, both with holding up his hands and making dolorous countenance, for his speech was gone for fear. 'Save him', said his chaplain, 'for he is a prince's son, and peradventure may do you good hereafter.' With that word, the Lord Clifford marked him and said: 'By God's blood, thy father slew mine, and so I will do thee and all thy kin', and with that word, struck the earl to the heart with his dagger, and bade his chaplain bear the earl's mother and brother word of what he had done, and said. In this act

Engraving by W.S. Stacey depicting the moment just before Clifford, with the words, 'thy father slew mine, and so I shall do thee and all thy kin . . .' murderously slew Edmund, Earl of Rutland, on Wakefield Chantry Bridge. His tutor, Sir Robert Aspall, pleads for the young earl's life. Though Aspall survived, Rutland did not, and was slain either on the bridge itself, or at a spot nearby. For the earl's murder and other infamous deeds, Clifford was to become known as 'The Butcher' and elsewhere as 'Black-Hearted' or 'Black-Faced Clifford'. (G. Wheeler)

the Lord Clifford was labelled a tyrant, and no gentleman; for the property of the lion, which is a furious and unreasonable beast, is to be cruel to them that withstand him, and gentle to such as prostrate or humiliate themselves before him. Yet this cruel Clifford and deadly Bloodsupper not content with this homicide, or child-killing . . .[2]

Worcester, by contrast, only briefly mentions Rutland's demise in his account of

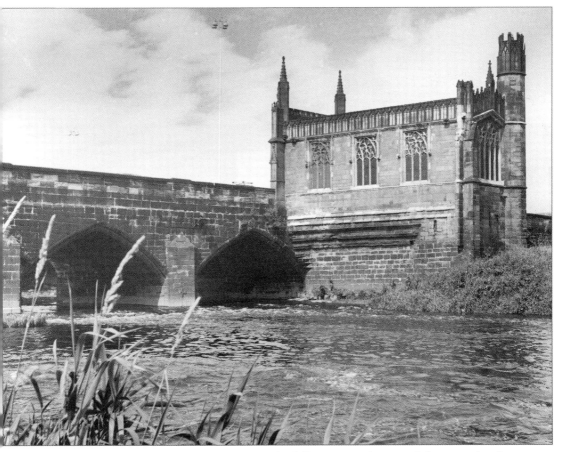

St Mary's Chapel on Wakefield Bridge. Note the different types of stonework demonstrating the degree of 'restoration' that the chapel went through in the last century. (G. Wheeler)

the battle: 'After the battle, Lord Clifford slew the young Earl of Rutland, the son of the Duke of York, as he was fleeing across the Bridge at Wakefield.'[3] This act of murder was also recorded by Stow as follows: 'The Lord Clifford perceiving where the Earl of Rutland was conveyed out of the field, by one of his father chaplains, and followed and overtook him, and stabbed him to death with a dagger as he kneeled before him.'[4]

The location of Rutland's death is hotly disputed. Many believed that he was captured on Wakefield Bridge itself,[5] while trying to gain sanctuary in the chapel that is built upon it. Leland, however, who visited the field of battle in 1544 wrote that Rutland was murdered: '. . . a little above the barres, beyond the Bridge going up into the Town of Wakefield that standith full fairely upon the clyving ground'.

Leland also stated that:

The commune saying is there, that the Erle wold have taken ther a poore Woman's House for socour, and she for fere shet the Dore and strait the Erle was killid. The Lord Clifford for killing of Men at this Batail was caullid the Boucher[6] . . .[7]

Leland also makes reference to a cross later being erected to mark the spot of Rutland's demise: 'At this place is set up a crosse in rei memoriam.'

It is not possible to ascertain whether he was referring to the cross erected to mark the location of the Duke of York's death, adjacent to Wakefield Green or a separate one marking the spot where Rutland is said to have been killed. If the latter is the case, then, unfortunately the exact location of this cross is not known for it certainly did not survive the test of time. However, Dr John Walker, who wrote a paper on the history of Wakefield, including the bridge and chapel, remarked that:

A cross existed at the bottom of Kirkgate, not far from the bridge, long before the battle of Wakefield, for in the will of Joan de Thorp, dated 12th April 1420, it is thus mentioned:

'I leave to the repair of the road between the bridge and the high cross at the end of Kirkgate, 3s. 4d.'

This shows that the cross was at some distance from the bridge and it was probably near to 'the barres' or gate at the end of Kirkgate. This cross may have been repaired or even rebuilt after the battle; in Dr Johnston's notes it is stated that the cross was erected after the battle, that 'it was taken away about 25 years ago, and set up in the Monday Market-place, but was pulled down and defaced in the [civil] wars'.[8]

As quoted above, Hall's chronicle refers to Rutland seeking, and being refused, sanctuary. As to the actual location of Rutland's death, I feel that there is sufficient information to prove that the earl and his tutor (who was more likely to have been his tutor in arms[9] than his tutor in educational or spiritual matters) were captured at some point beyond the bridge. Indeed Barrett, in his account of the battle, goes further and says 'near that building called "Six Chimneys" in Kirkgate,[10] Wakefield, is locally supposed to mark the site of Rutland's death . . . the "Six Chimneys" itself, however, stands where it did on the day of the fight, and is the only contemporary building remaining in the city.'[11, 12]

As to Rutland being only a boy of twelve, thus compounding the 'murderous act', this is, in fact, untrue, for William of Worcester chronicles the birth of all of the Duke of York's children as follows:

Anna, Countess of Exeter, born at Fotheringhay, on Monday 10 August 1439
Henry, born at Hatfield, on Friday 10 February 1441
Edward, Earl of March, born at Rouen, on Saturday 28 April 1442
Edmund, Earl of Rutland, born at Rouen, on Friday 17 May 1443
Elizabeth, born at Rouen, on Saturday 22 April 1444
Margaret, born at Fotheringhay, on Tuesday 3 May 1446

The 'Six Chimneys' building, Kirkgate, Wakefield. Some people believe that this is the true spot where the Earl of Rutland met his death.

William, born at Fotheringhay, on Friday 7 July 1447
John, born at Neyte, on Thursday 7 November 1448
George, Duke of Clarence, born in Ireland, on Tuesday 21 October 1449
Thomas, born 1450
Richard, Duke of Gloucester, born at Fotheringhay, on Monday 2 October 1452
Ursula, born at Fotheringhay, on Sunday 20 July 1455.[13]

This proves that the Earl of Rutland was seventeen in 1460. Markham's account of the battle goes even further and mentions other details about the Duke of York's family:

In the year of the battle of Wakefield, the Duke of York had reached the age of 48; and had twelve children by his wife Duchess Cicely. Of these the two elder daughters were already married to Lancastrian husbands, the Dukes of Exeter and Suffolk; and five had died young. Two princes [were] approaching man's estate and the three children were still with their parents. Edward, the Earl of March, was born at Rouen in 1442. Edmund, the Earl of Rutland, was also born at Rouen in 1443. There was a year and a few days between them. They seem to have been brought up as twins. They played and studied together, and wrote joint letters to their father.

*Detail of the signatures of Edward and Edmund on a letter written
at Ludlow Castle to their father, Richard Duke of York.*

Two of these letters have been preserved, written when the boys were 12 and
11 years old respectively. In one they say:

'We thanke your noblesse and good ffadurhod for our grene gownes nowe
late sende unto us to our grete comfort: beseeching your good lordeship that we
might have summe fyne bonetts sende un to us by the next sure messig, for
necessitie so requireth.'

This letter was written from the duke's castle at Ludlow. In the next, dated
June 3rd 1454, they say:

'If it please your Highness to know of our welfare at the making of this letter, we
were in good health of body thanked be God; beseeching your good and gracious
fatherhood of your daily blessing. And where ye command us, by your said letters,
to attend specially to our learning in our young age, please it your Highness to wit,
that we have attended our learning since we came hither, and shall hereafter, by
which we trust to God your gracious Lordship that it may please you to send us
Harry Lovedeyne, clerk of your kitchen, whose service is to us right agreeable: and
we will send you John Boys to wait on your good Lordship.'

One of these bright young princes was destined to meet his death just as he was
entering manhood, at the fateful battle of Wakefield.[14]

It is likely that the young earl and his tutor were among a number of Yorkists
who tried to escape across the river via the bridge. William Gregory describes
Rutland as 'one of the best disposed Lords in this land'; he was certainly well
versed in the use of arms and it seems likely that he fought his way during the
rout to the place where he was captured. It is not to be doubted that it was at
Clifford's hand that Rutland met his death. Clifford certainly had a motive, his
own father having been killed by the Yorkists five years previously at the battle of
St Albans, and it was said that 'the sight of any of the house of York, was as a fury
to torment his soul'. The fate of the earl's tutor, Sir Robert Aspall, is not recorded.

The remains of the bailey at Pontefract Castle. On this spot the Earl of Salisbury and several other Yorkist leaders were executed, on 31 December 1460, after being captured at the battle of Wakefield the previous day. (Author's collection)

THE FATE OF THE EARL OF SALISBURY

Stanfield, who wrote about the battle of Wakefield in a paper read before the Wakefield Photographic Society in 1891, claimed that:

> Bonfires were lighted after the battle, and by the fierce glare of these the conquerors buried the bodies of the slain in the grounds of the castle and on the field of battle. A letter written at the time by a son who visited the bloody field in search of the dead body of his father says that, 'At midnight the kindly snow fell like a mantle on the dead, and covered the rueful faces staring so fiercely up to heaven.'[15]

It was during this period, some time after the battle, so it is said, that the Earl of Salisbury, who had escaped from the carnage, was captured by an unnamed servant of Andrew Trollope. This is supported by Worcester, who chronicled it as follows: '. . . and in the same night the Earl of Salisbury was captured by a follower of Sir Andrew Trollope'.[16] It is not recorded how Salisbury managed to escape the field. But, either that same night or the following day, along with Sir Ralph Stanley, Walter Lymbrike, John Harrow and Captain Hanson, who had also been captured, he was taken to Pontefract Castle. It is generally agreed that the Lancastrians planned to spare his life in return for a large ransom, a point supported by the words of the chronicler Vergil (p. 356). However, as William of Worcester went on to describe, the Earl of Salisbury and the other prisoners were 'on the morrow beheaded by the Bastard of Exeter at Pontefract'.[17] Other chroniclers, including Stow, told it rather differently. Stow said:

> The Earl of Salisbury had the grant of his life for a great ransom, but that the common people at Pontefract, who loved him not,[18] took him out of the castle by violence and smote off his head.[19]

However, the author of *An English Chronicle of the reigns of Richard II, Henry IV, V, VI* claimed:

> The Earl of Salisbury was taken alive, and led by the said Duke of Somerset to the castle of Pomfret, and for a great sum of money that he should have paid for grant of his life. But the common people of the county which loved him not, took him from the castle by violence and smote off his head.[20]

Edward Hall is more direct:

> . . . caused the Earl of Salisbury, with all the other prisoners, to be sent to Pontefract and there to be beheaded.[21]

Although some claimed it was the 'Bastard of Exeter' – William Holland, the illegitimate son of Sir Henry Holland, Duke of Exeter – and not the 'common people' who dragged the Earl of Salisbury to his death, it is only William of Worcester who names Salisbury's murderer. It is difficult to prove conclusively, however, whether it was the 'common folk', the 'Bastard of Exeter' or a third party who instigated Salisbury's execution.[22]

THE LANCASTRIAN RETURN TO YORK

What followed during the hours immediately after the battle is not clear. Other than the capture of the Earl of Salisbury, his subsequent execution the following day, and the death of the Earl of Rutland, the actions of the victorious Lancastrians are not recorded in detail by the chroniclers. We know that Sandal Castle was pillaged, although there must have been precious little worth taking. Once the battlefield had been cleared of the debris of battle, the various nobles present, no doubt still elated after their victory, knighted a number of their followers, before the victorious Lancastrian army returned to Pontefract Castle. But at some point during this period, the bodies of the Yorkist commanders were subjected to an act of shocking barbarity, appalling even by the standards of that ruthless age. It was chronicled by Hall as follows:

> Yet this cruel Clifford and deadly Bloodsupper not content with this homicide, or child-killing [Rutland's murder] came to the place where the dead corpse of the Duke of York lay, and caused his head to be stricken off, and set upon it a crown of paper, and so fixed it on a pole . . .[23]

*'Now looks he like a king', engraving by Byam Shaw for the Chiswick Shakespeare series (1901).
A dramatic version of the captive York, restrained by the Earl of Northumberland and Clifford
before a triumphant Margaret of Anjou. In reality, Margaret was not at the battlefield and it is
unlikely that the Duke of York was captured. He clearly died during the battle itself. (G. Wheeler)*

Polydore Vergil simply records: 'Richard, erle of Salisbury, another head of that faction, was amongst other taken, who were beheaded soon after, and their heads, put upon stakes',[24] while according to Stow: 'The same Lord Clifford not satisfied herewith, came to the place where the dead corps of the Duke of York lay, and caused his head to be stricken off, and set on it a crown of paper and fixed it on a pole.'[25]

After this, the Lancastrians set off towards York, intent on being reunited with Margaret of Anjou, who had remained all this time in Scotland gathering support and raising an army of mercenaries. Whether the Duke of Somerset sent a message to Margaret, informing her of their victory and advising her of the meeting place, or whether the rendezvous was preordained is hard to say. Some historians have claimed that Margaret was present at the battle of Wakefield, or at least was nearby, despite all the evidence that points to her having been in Scotland throughout. It is my opinion that Shakespeare's dramatic licence in describing the 'execution' of the Duke of York in Queen Margaret's presence is the fundamental reason behind this thinking. However, in all fairness, despite Shakespeare's influence, more modern-day historians could be forgiven for this mistake because some of the contemporary chroniclers, including Stow (p. 685) and Edward Hall (pp. 250–1) do in fact mention Margaret's presence at Wakefield. Both Hall and Stow record that Clifford went to the queen with the severed head of York. Hall said:

> . . . and presented it to the queen, not lying far from the field, in great despite, and much derision, saying: 'Madam, your war is done, here is your king's ransom', at which present, was much joy, and great rejoicing, but many laughed then that sore lamented after – as the queen herself, and her son. And many were glad then of other men's deaths, not knowing that their own was near at hand – as the Lord Clifford, and other . . .[26]

Stow's version is very similar: 'and presented it to the queen, not lying far from the field. The duke's head with the Earl of Salisbury's were set upon a gate of York.'[27] My view is that if this occurred at all, then it happened when Margaret entered York. There is no doubt that the severed heads of York, Salisbury and several other Yorkist commanders (namely Lymbrike, Stanley, Bourchier, Thomas Harrington, William Parr, Pickering, Harrow and Hanson), were displayed around York. William of Worcester recorded that the heads were 'affixed in various parts of York, whilst a paper crown was placed in derision on the head of the Duke of York'.[28] Polydore Vergil wrote that the heads 'were carried to Yorke for a spectacle to the people, and a terror to the rest of their adversaryes'.[29]

The Duke of York's head was placed above Micklegate Bar and the vengeful Queen Margaret ordered that a sign be placed below it, on which was written: 'Let York overlook the town of York.' It is also said that she instructed that sufficient space should be left between the heads of Salisbury and Hanson for the heads of the Earl of Warwick and the Earl of March. This is mentioned by the chronicler Stow (p. 413) and by the latter-day historian Leadman (p. 357). Finally

Micklegate Bar, York. Upon the Lancastrian arrival at the city of York, the severed heads of the Duke of York and the Earl of Salisbury and several other Yorkist leaders were impaled on spikes and set above this gate. It is also said that upon the head of the Duke of York was placed a paper crown and below it a sign, upon which were written the words 'Let York overlook the town of York'. (G. Wheeler)

a paper crown was affixed to the head of the Duke of York, in mocking reference to his claim to the throne. This was the final act of the Wakefield campaign – although the Wars of the Roses would continue for another three decades.

In the following years the outrages committed against the Duke of York, the Earl of Rutland and the Earl of Salisbury greatly aggravated the hatred felt by many people, commoners and nobility alike, against Queen Margaret and her Lancastrian commanders. It also brought about a distinct change in the treatment of prisoners captured during subsequent battles. The system of ransoming knights for money was replaced by wholesale slaughter, murder and revenge, and in future years the Yorkists and Lancastrians were to prove themselves equally ruthless in their treatment of nobles captured on the field of battle. After the battle of St Albans, King Henry VI himself promised Sir Thomas Kyriell and Lord Bonville pardon if they stayed to protect him during the Yorkist rout. Yet not even their king's word was sufficient to spare Kyriell and Bonville from Lancastrian vengeance and both were executed shortly afterwards. After the battle of Towton, the Yorkists executed some sixty nobles who had been captured during the battle. After the battle of Hexham in 1464, John Neville (then Lord Montagu, later Earl of Northumberland), finally captured Henry Beaufort, Duke of Somerset, and had him executed – no doubt in revenge for the deaths of his father, the Earl of Salisbury, and his brother, Thomas Neville, at Wakefield. The Earl of March, later Edward IV, was equally ruthless in the year after Wakefield. After his victory at the battle of Mortimer's Cross he ordered the execution of Owen Tudor and several other Lancastrian nobles who had been captured during the battle. After the battle of Tewkesbury in 1471 Edward finally destroyed the last vestiges of Lancastrian resistance and had many of the captured Lancastrians executed, despite having previously granted them pardon. The most notable of these was Edmund Beaufort, Duke of Somerset, the brother of Henry, Duke of Somerset, who had fought at Wakefield. This act all but completed the extermination of the Beaufort family.

CHAPTER SEVEN

The Battlefield – Present

. . . A Walk about Wakefield . . .

THE CASTLE

Today little remains of the battlefield of 1460 and there are only a handful of clues to indicate what took place here 500 years ago. The castle itself is a mere shadow of its former self, as it was utterly destroyed at the end of the English Civil War (1646) on the orders of Parliament, after its Royalist garrison had finally surrendered in 1645. Many of the buildings had been destroyed by artillery fire during the siege, and most of the stonework (some of which had fallen into the ditches surrounding the castle), was removed in subsequent years, along with any other recyclable materials. During the siege, the cross erected as a memorial to the death of the Duke of York, allegedly on the spot where he fell, was also destroyed.[1]

In recent years housing estates, commercial developments and a park have all but covered what was known as Sandal Common. However, a very small portion of it, later known as Wakefield Green, still remains. If we start at the castle, we can reconstruct the battlefield of 'yesterday' by walking the developed site of it today. The castle can be easily located near to the M1 motorway by the 'Denby Dale' turn-off (Junction 39). In fact, motorists travelling either north or south can clearly see the castle from the motorway. The site itself can be found off the A61, Barnsley road, and can be easily accessed by turning on to Manygates Lane, where the lane intersects with the A61. Fortunately there are adequate car parking facilities on site.

Between 1964 and 1973 Wakefield City Council, Wakefield Historical Society and the University of Leeds joined forces to begin the excavation of Sandal Castle, under the direction of Phil Mayes and Lawrence Butler. The fact that the castle remains can be viewed today is testament to the painstaking work they carried out. However, the results of this recent excavation are too far-reaching and extensive to be recounted here; for a full analysis read *Sandal Castle – Wakefield*, by Lawrence Butler (Wakefield Historical Publications, 1991). However, they were not the first to make a study of the castle – for many years it has been a favourite location for local artists, poets, historians and archaeologists, but there has also been at least one other 'professional' study of Sandal Castle. With regards to this earlier excavation, and the subsequent interest in the castle ruins, Butler wrote:

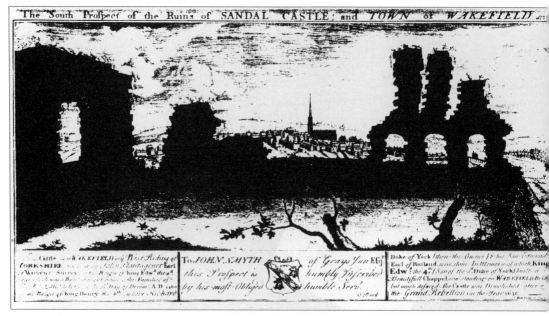

Sandal Castle and Wakefield, engraving by Samuel Buck (drawn in 1722).

The castle owners, the Neville family of Chevet, made no use of '. . . one demolished or ruinus Buildinge called Sandal . . .', nor did the subsequent owners the Pilkingtons who held it after 1753. Instead it became a subject of occasional antiquarian interest, of poetic and artistic inspiration and a place of relaxation for the steadily growing number of Wakefield's inhabitants. It twice attracted the attention of antiquarians: the earlier occasion was when it was drawn by Samuel Buck in 1719 or 1722 as the foreground ruins to a prospect of Wakefield to the south; this view was published in 1774. The second occasion was the publication of an engraving by George Vertue in 1753 showing the Elizabethan drawing among the Duchy of Lancaster surveys; other drawings from these surveys were published as *Vetusta Monumenta* ('Ancient Monuments'). The harsh shading of the engraving and the disproportionate size of the nearby trees have made this a less attractive depiction of the castle than that by Buck . . .

. . . the first excavation in 1869 was carried out by the Yorkshire Archaeological Society, then Huddersfield based, who had visited the castle in 1869 but the first serious attempt at exploration was not until 1893 when a local historian, J.W. Walker [and] a mining engineer, H.S. Childe, conducted a period excavation. Workmen were engaged for three months to dig trenches to confirm the evidence of the Elizabethan drawing . . .

. . . Walker published his work promptly in 1895; he added many historical references and illustrated a medieval ring and a seal found in the locality. He

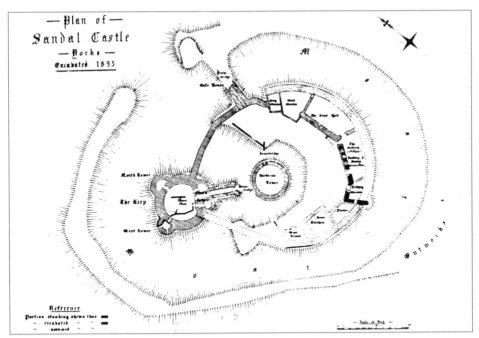

Dr W. Walker's excavation plan of Sandal Castle 1893, from his History of Wakefield.

continued to maintain an interest in the castle and in his fuller though discursive 'History of Wakefield' (1934; 2nd edition 1939) he added a little more information.[2]

At the castle today, there is nothing to commemorate the battle of Wakefield and unless visitors have previous knowledge of what transpired, then they would be none the wiser in viewing the ruins. However, the climb to the highest point of the mound where the keep once stood is rewarded by an impressive view of the surrounding countryside. Open farmland lies to the west and south, interspersed with modern developments including a supermarket complex and a watersports park. The water park is called 'Pugneys Country Park' and is named after the area on which the man-made lake was created, 'The Pugnays'. In early fifteenth-century manor rolls this area is referred to as 'The Pukenills', while on the earliest Ordnance Survey map (1850) it is called 'Pugnells'. It is said that part of the battle was fought over this ground, although it is probably more correct to say that the area formed part of the wooded areas where some of the Lancastrians concealed themselves before the battle. Visible to the north-west, beyond the river, is a tree-covered mound, which is the site of Lawe Hill (*see* p. 95).

To the north is Wakefield and to the east Sandal, which has now been swallowed up by the expanding metropolis of Wakefield. Other than an expanse of farmland which runs from the ruins of the castle for some 300–400 yards in a northerly direction, the view of what was the battlefield is totally obscured by the

The Cock and Bottle public house. The building still retains its original fire plate, placed high up on the wall near the eaves, facing the road. It is now a private house. (Author's collection)

housing and commercial development which today makes up two of Wakefield's suburbs, Portobello and Belle Vue (also called Belle Isle).

To the south-east of the castle is an unusual earthwork, a depression shaped like an orange segment. This earthwork was built as a redoubt to help defend the castle during the English Civil War and at that time would have housed several pieces of ordnance, although later excavations produced no evidence to show that the defenders of the castle had any heavy weapons.

Nothing now remains of the vast stretches of woodland which used to lie to both east and west of Sandal Castle. Because of this, and because of the later development of the site, it requires a vivid imagination to recreate the view that the Duke of York would have seen from this same spot in December 1460.

COCK AND BOTTLE LANE

Having viewed the battlefield from this vantage point, one should then return to the car park and walk down Manygates Lane towards the city of Wakefield. After a short walk along the narrow road, enclosed on either side by modern housing, one reaches Castle Mount, a residential nursing home. Just before it, on the left-

A view of the battlefield as described by the advocates of School B, photographed from the high ground upon which Sandal Castle stands. (Author's collection)

hand side of the road between the nursing home and Castle Road West, is a short row of terraced houses. Before being converted to residential accommodation, these buildings were a single property, the Cock and Bottle public house. Manygates Lane was originally called after this public house and was for many years known as Cock and Bottle Lane. The pub was a stopping place for coaches using the turnpike road but lost its licence in 1866, and was subsequently converted into a residential block.

This site was also the birthplace in 1758 of George Scholry, who later became Lord Mayor of London and an alderman of that city. Scholry made his wealth both through trade as a merchant and by marriage, and was a local benefactor – in his will he left £10,000 to the poor of Wakefield.

THE BATTLEFIELDS

Turn left into Castle Road West, which is situated on the left-hand side of the road before the nursing home. After a short distance the road becomes a track, which leads to open ground just beyond some houses on the right. From this spot we are able to view what I believe is the battlefield, albeit covered with modern housing. It also offers a good opportunity to observe the steep gradient from Sandal Castle down towards Wakefield Green. In my opinion, this view also supports the 'School B' argument proposed by Brooke and others that the battle was fought 'in the plain' between the high ground at Sandal and the high ground just south of the River Calder.

Continue along the track as it circumnavigates the open ground previously observed from the castle. The track soon straightens out into Milnthorpe Lane, which very closely follows the route of the old medieval road to Wakefield. Here, just beyond the built-up area, there is a footpath on the right, which leads off westwards between the field and the housing estate, towards the river. From a point halfway along the path, the former site of Wakefield's Infectious Diseases Hospital can be seen to the north. This hospital is clearly shown on the Ordnance Survey map of 1914, and at that time it was suitably located well away from the town of Wakefield. Supporters of 'School A' believe that the battlefield is on this spot and to the right of the path as it descends here towards the river.

PORTOBELLO HOUSE

At the point where the footpath meets the brick bridge over the drain, turn north (right), and walk along the dirt road parallel to the river until you reach the open grassland to the left, just before the housing estate. Pugneys Road leads off from this point. About 50 yards further on is the entrance into Riverside Villas.

Portobello House and its gardens were located between the rear of this building and Riverside Villas. In digging the cellars and foundations for these houses during the nineteenth century there were found the remains of spurs, swords and armour, said to have come from the battle of Wakefield. (Author's collection)

Portobello House used to stand between this point and the Portobello public house, some 50 yards further along Pugneys Road (where it joins with Portobello Road). In the course of its construction in 1825, various artefacts believed to be connected with the battle were discovered here, but sadly none of them can today be viewed by the modern historian. Only one item is said to survive, a sword apparently found a little way to the south of the site of Portobello House. Little is known about this sword, and its whereabouts are now unknown; it was sold at Christie's in April 1966 to an anonymous buyer. It had previously been in the collection of H.C. Haldane of Clarke Hall, who wrote that the sword was 'dug up a few years ago during the operation of cutting a main drain near the site of the battle of Wakefield'.[3] Richard Knowles described the sword as follows:

> [the sword] . . . is of unusual sort, not a knightly weapon, but single edged, possibly cut down from a larger blade. It has a curious guard with an extension of the cross guard protecting the back of the hand. Whilst this is a late medieval form, some concern may be felt that this particular type of sword has tended to be dated by the Wakefield example despite its rather doubtful provenance.[4]

Nothing now remains of Portobello House and its surrounding gardens, but its site is significant in determining where the battle was fought.

TOWARDS WAKEFIELD BRIDGE

If we leave this estate behind us, and continue our walk down Portobello Road, the road eventually merges with the A61 – or as Brooke called it – the Barnsley turnpike road. If we continue towards the centre of Wakefield, shortly there will come into view, on the far side of the road, the old Wakefield Bridge – the alleged site of the death of the Earl of Rutland.

While travelling towards the bridge, a little beyond where Portobello Road meets the A61, we will pass on the left hand side of the road the bus station (which is clearly visible on the road side). It is between these two points, in my opinion, that the Lancastrian right flank was situated at the start of the battle. Almost opposite this location is the turning into Belle Vue Avenue, and a little to the south of this are the turnings into Bromley Mount and Welbeck Street. Along a line cutting through these roads and extending on towards the cemetery, which lies to the east of Sugar Lane, the Lancastrian front was drawn up.

On reaching the bridge, pause for a moment to make a comparison between the battlefield that Brooke viewed in 1852, and which still retained its rural aspect, and that which Freeman saw some fifty years later in 1894. By this time the view had already changed considerably, for he wrote:

> Standing on the bridge and looking eastwards, westwards, and southwards, as far as the smoke of Wakefield chimneys will let us look anyway, several special points may be made out among the low and wooded hills which rise on either side . . .

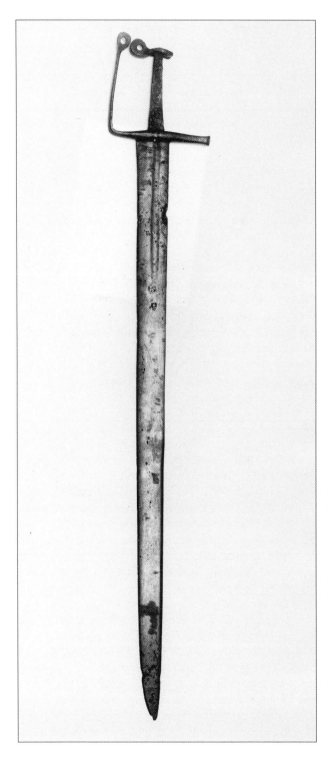

The 'Wakefield Sword', said to have been found to the south of Portobello House during the process of digging a drain. Little is known of this sword other than after its discovery it formed part of a collection owned by H.C. Haldane, of Clarke Hall. It was sold at Christie's in April 1966 to an anonymous buyer, after which its location was lost. The sword itself is an extremely rare archer's single-edge sword of a type illustrated in the Beauchamp Pageant. (Author's collection; photo: Christie's, London)

Freeman described one of his special points thus:

> To the east, close above the right bank [south] of the river, rises the hill crowned by the picturesque Elizabethan mansion of the Heath, which, as far as we know, does not connect itself of the battle.[5]

LAWE HILL

Freeman went on:

> But to the west, on the left hand [north] bank of the river, lies the high ground of Thornes and Lupsett, and there is one special point which is said to have played a part in the battle, and which at all events is remarkable on its own account. This is the small peaked hill just outside the park of Thornes, immediately overlooking the town to the west, which bears the name varied by endless local spellings, of Lawe or Lowe Hill.
>
> The former part of the name is of course the same as that which is found in the names of many heights in Northern Britain, the Old-English *hloew*, the Gothic *hlaiv*, the word used by Ulfilas for the holy tomb, and which lives in a most corrupted shape in the *Cuckamsley*, the *Cwichelmeshloew*, to Berkshire topography.
>
> A central mound, seemingly, like so many others, a natural mound raised and improved by art and surrounded by a deep ditch, crowns a series of slighter fortifications on the slope of the hill. The name, purely descriptive and not connected with any Teutonic eponyms, may suggest that it is the work of the conquered Welsh, which the English conquerors of the Brigantian land found in much the same state as it is now.
>
> It is a hill fort which might have grown into a castle or into a city, but which the caprice of human affairs has left untouched among the surrounding dwellings of man. The very meaning of its name has been forgotten; the word *hloew* ceased to carry any meaning to modern ears, and, as so happens, another word of the same meaning was added as an explanatory description of the word which had passed into a unintelligible proper name.
>
> This Lowe or Lawe Hill, already so distinguished in the sixteenth century, has been thought, we know not exactly on what authority, to have been the headquarters of the Lancastrian side. It is more certain that it connects itself most temptingly with the spot on the other side of the river which undoubtedly was the headquarters of the Yorkists . . .
>
> . . . Now there would seem to be thus much of truth in the legend, that a process actually did take place at Sandal which did not, though it might almost have been looked for, take place at Lawe Hill. A primeval fortress was taken advantage of in the building of a medieval castle. In the present state of the place primeval and mediaeval works are hopelessly confounded, or rather, as so often happens, the earlier works have survived the later.[6]

Despite the fact that this hill 'connects itself most temptingly with the spot on the other side of the river', in my opinion this hill had absolutely nothing to do with the battle. Indeed one can conclude that precisely because it was so far away from the river crossing it is extremely unlikely to have been used as a command post for the Lancastrians. Their commanders would undoubtedly have remained close to the rank and file not only during the battle itself but also in the build-up to it. Therefore it is my belief that in respect to this engagement, the hill had no strategic value whatsoever. The only possible connection with the campaign would have been when the Yorkists first arrived at Wakefield. Since not all of the duke's men could be housed at Sandal, then some of those who chose to remain close to the town may have used the hill as a natural shelter on which to bivouac.

THE BRIDGE AND CHAPEL

Putting this aside, we come to the bridge and the chapel built upon it. We are fortunate in being able to study the very detailed account of Dr John Walker, whose work remains authoritative even today. In recounting the chapel's history he wrote:

> The idea that the chapel was built after the battle of Wakefield, by Edward IV, that the masses might be said for the souls of those who fell in the fray, especially for his father – the Duke of York, and his brother – the Earl of Rutland, has long held possession in the public's mind, but the impression is a totally erroneous one[7] . . . We have no knowledge as to when the first bridge was built over the Calder at this place, but on February 18th 1342 Edward III granted the bailiffs of the town of Wakefield tollage for three years on all goods for sale and animals passing over the bridge '. . . as a help towards the repairs and improvements of the said bridge, which is now rent and broken . . .'[8]
>
> I think it very possible that when the bailiffs of the town examined the bridge and applied for help in 1342, they saw that a new bridge was required and that at this time the suggestion was first made that a chapel in honour of the Blessed Virgin Mary should be erected by the townsfolk, as was done on so many other bridges during this century. . . . If my surmise be correct, that it was about this time that the plans were first discussed, doubtless the period which elapsed before the building was commenced would be spent in collecting funds. The construction of the bridge started soon after 1342, when the right of tollage was granted to the bailiffs . . .
>
> There are several proofs showing that the erection and endowment of this bridge-chapel were undertaken and completed by the townsfolk of Wakefield.
>
> The guilds of the town probably contributed freely to this work, stimulated by the priests who served at the various chantry-altars in their parish church, two of whom – William Bull and William Kay – were among those who applied for the king's licence in 1357.
>
> The basement of the chapel was undoubtedly built at the same time as the bridge, for the masonry of the two is bonded together, and the walls of the chapel and the piers of the bridge are constructed of the same sandstone.[9]

It appears that the building of the bridge and chapel was delayed, as Wakefield, like so many other towns, recovered from the ravages of the Black Death.

The chapel on the bridge at Wakefield. Painting by R.R. Reinagle RA (1794) showing the chapel before restoration. (G. Wheeler)

However, the chapel was completed and was being serviced by two resident chaplains by 1357. In his paper on the history of the chapel, Walker devotes much of his work to the daily running of the chantry and gives details of many of the events that occurred over the years in its colourful history. The following extract gives an account of the later history of the chapel and tells how it fell into disuse:

> When in 1534, Henry VIII sent commissioners throughout the kingdom to compile the Valor Ecclesiasticus, in order that he might know the value of his first-fruits of all benefices, the chantry in this chapel was returned as an annual value of £12 8s. 11d and the two priests Richard Seal and Tristram Harton, had each an income of £6 3s. 7d. The Act for the dissolution of chantries was passed in the 37th year of the reign of Henry VIII [1545] . . .

The chapel then passed through several private hands until it was:

> . . . conveyed to the trustees of the general poor of Wakefield, now known as the governors of the charities; but the deed making it over to them was probably lost when the Parliamentarian soldiers under Sir Thomas Fairfax broke into the room over the south porch of the parish church, after the capture of Wakefield

on Whit-Sunday morning, May 21st 1643, and destroyed many of the papers kept there by the governors.

The trustees of the general poor of Wakefield [the governors] let out the Chapel to various tenants . . .[10]

From this point on, it appears that the chapel was used for many different types of commercial ventures: at different times it served variously as a warehouse, a clothes dealer's shop, a corn factor's office and a cheese-maker's premises. All these businesses benefited from the bridge's key trading location. It was only in the mid-1800s that a serious attempt was made to revive the chapel's original function as a place of religious worship. The Revd Samuel Sharp, then vicar of Wakefield, first suggested a scheme to restore the chapel to its former use. At the time, the chapel still belonged to the Governors of Wakefield Charities, although for many years it had been leased to the county magistrates, who had at least attempted to keep it in some degree of repair even after letting it out to tenants. On behalf of the governors, an application was made to the magistrates to give up possession of the building, and in order to facilitate this, the following order was made:

> The Rev Samuel Sharp, having applied on behalf of the governors of the Wakefield Charities, for possession of the chapel on Wakefield Bridge, now in lease to the magistrates of the Riding at the yearly rent of sixpence, ordered that the clerk of the Peace give immediate notice to the under-tenants to quit the premises in order that the possession may be given to the Governors as soon as possible.

It is signed E. Lascelles, Chairman.[11]

Not content with this, the industrious Revd Sharp, in pursuit of his goal, persuaded his fellow governors to hand over the chapel to the Commissioners for building additional churches, and the following 'resolution' is entered on the minutes for the meeting that they held on 24 October 1842: 'That the Chapel on the Bridge be conveyed to Her Majesty's Commissioners, for building and promoting the building of additional churches in populous parishes, according to the provisions of the 3rd Geo. IV. chap 72.'

Several of the local nobility and landed gentry now came forward to assist with the cost of restoring the building and, after some debate, the restoration plan submitted by Mr G.G. Scott (later Sir Gilbert Scott) was adopted. There then began the complete rebuilding, rather than restoration, of the chapel. Most of the building above basement level was pulled down and replaced, so that what we see now is, alas, only a shadow of the original. The new building is said to be a replica of the original, but as Scott remarked in later years, realizing his error:

> It was an evil hour when I relented, yielded and allowed a new front in Caen stone in place of the weather-beaten old stone . . . I never repented it but once, and that has been ever since. I think of this with the utmost shame and chagrin.[12]

The original front of the bridge chapel preserved in the grounds of Kettlethorpe Hall. Compare this to Reinagle's painting shown on page 97. (G. Wheeler)

Scott was so concerned that his earlier error of judgement should be put right that he offered to contribute personally to restoring the original west front from its new home in the grounds of Kettlethorpe Hall, where it had been erected after being purchased by the Hon. George Chapple Norton in 1847. However, this plan came to nothing and he died, unable to put right the wrong he felt he had committed.

The chapel reopened on Easter Sunday, 22 April 1848, and services are still held there, as can be seen from the plaque on the door. For those who require a descriptive account of the chapel, again, we are fortunate to have Walker's work to refer to. He described the chapel in its heyday as follows:

> The bridge over the Calder at Wakefield consists of nine arches; the eastern side with its four ribbed, pointed arches, having been built as I believe, about 1342; the width at that time being only about sixteen feet between the parapets. The foundations of the chapel were laid on a small island in the middle of the river, against and forming part of the northern pier of the central arch.
>
> The material used in the building was sandstone, probably from the quarry in the Goodybower, on the north side of the parish church, which stone was also used for the alterations of that edifice in the fourteenth century. This

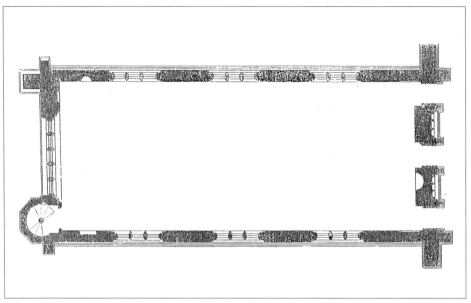

Plan of the ground floor of the chapel on Wakefield Bridge.

quarry is mentioned in the Towneley Mystery Plays. At a few feet above the foundations the building on each side increases in width by means of corbel courses, which spring from the lower walls, and on which the whole weight of the side walls of the fabric rest.

The external measurements were length 50 feet, width 25 feet, height, up to the top of the battlements, 36 feet. The west front terminated at either end in a buttress, between which were five compartments or panels, which extended the whole height of the edifice, and were separated from each other by slender buttresses. The five arches were alike in design, with crocketed labels, above which were gabled pediments, the tympana and spandrels having been covered with tracery.

Three of these arches were originally doorways, the other two having been filled with tracery to resemble blank windows. Below the parapet was a deep weathering surmounted by battlements. The fivefold division of the west front was carried through into the parapet, which consisted of five panels of sculpture, each panel surmounted by a canopy of three cinquefoil arches, above which were the battlements. Each of these panels contained a sculptured representation of one of the five glorious mysteries of the Rosary: the Annunciation to the Virgin by the Angel Gabriel; the Nativity; the Resurrection; the Ascension; and the Coronation of the Virgin.

At each side of the chapel were three square-headed windows, with labels suspended from the cornice above, reaching half-way down the window, terminating in carved heads. These windows were of three lights with a

A representation of the sculpture of the Resurrection in the chapel.

beautiful head of flowing tracery. At the east end of the south side was, in addition to and at a higher level than the other windows, a small two-light 'high sided' window, which has been completely overlooked in the rebuilding the chapel. This window was probably contemporary with the rest of the building, and was intended for the exhibition of a light at night to travellers approaching the bridge from the south side, and would be extremely useful at a time when the land there was unenclosed. Possibly the light which was always burning before the image of the Virgin in the niche in the east wall served this double purpose, at any rate the position of the window would allow for this.

The north-east angle contained the staircase to the bell turret, which was octagonal in form, the walls finishing in a richly panelled parapet; the turret itself terminated in a crown of flying buttresses, and originally contained two bells. The east window was of six lights, not being square-headed as all the other windows were, but fitted to the pedimental lines of the roof, which was of wood covered with lead. Beneath the eastern third of the building was a sacristy

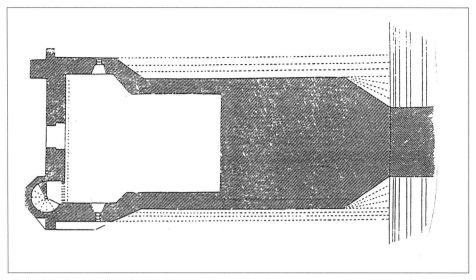

Plan of the basement level of the chapel.

reached by a stair in continuation of that from the roof, and only lighted by small loop window.[13]

The interior of the chapel today bears no resemblance to its original condition. Again Walker gives a description of what he believes it would have looked like at its height:

> On entering the chapel in the fifteenth century the wayfarer would look upon a somewhat different arrangement to that which would now meets the eye of a visitor. Immediately to the left of the central door was a recess in the wall, in which was a holy water stoup. The sanctuary was only raised a single step above the ordinary floor level. Beneath the east window stood a stone altar, marked with five crosses; the eye being carried from the rich altar frontal would ultimately rest upon the crucifix of precious metal, probably studded with gems.
>
> During the sacrifice of the Mass the plate required for that office might be seen, the chalice, paten and cruets of silver, richly chased and ornamented. Within a richly carved niche in the east wall of the chapel, and south of the altar, on a raised pedestal stood a figure of our Lady, to whom the chapel was dedicated. Above her head was a ribbed projecting canopy, terminating in a spire, and ornamented with pinnacles and crockets. In all probability, the Virgin was represented standing as the happy mother, with her babe on her left arm, wearing a royal crown, made of silver.
>
> Before this image a lamp, continually burning, would be suspended from the

ceiling, and as already mentioned, would be seen through the high side window. The piscina in the south wall was also richly carved but before the so-called restoration only a fragment of it remained, though sufficient to show its beauty. In the north wall, within the sanctuary, was a recess, which was probably used as an aumbry and had doors, so that the sacred vessels might be locked up when not in use. On the north side of the altar a doorway opened upon the staircase to the sacristy, which served as a vestry for the priests.

Paintings adorned the walls, traces of which could be seen before the demolition of the building, but now only in the carved work about the niche which contained the figure of the Virgin. Doubtless the windows were filled with painted glass, which, when the sun shone through them, would present a brilliant aspect, for this was the age of real glass painting. Possibly the east window depicted the Annunciation with the assumption or coronation of the Virgin, whilst the side window set forth scenes from the mystery of the Rosary.[14]

WAKEFIELD GREEN

Once the bridge and chapel have been viewed sufficiently to satisfy the reader's curiosity, then one option is to cross the bridge and walk to Thornes Park for a closer look at Lawe Hill. Otherwise, we should begin to retrace our steps. On the return to Wakefield, it should be borne in mind that this is the area of Wakefield that Brooke called the 'Fall Ings'. On his visit to Wakefield in 1852 he remarked that 'it has acquired the name Fall Ings, according to tradition, from great numbers who fell there, in the battle'.[15] This is probably where the Lancastrians caught up with many of the fleeing Yorkist troops during the rout. It is likely that many Yorkists died here, caught in the open ground as they tried to reach the crossing over the Calder.

Upon reaching Portobello Road, instead of turning towards the site of Portobello House, continue along the A61 as far as Manygates Lane. Turn onto the Lane and continue along it until you reach the railway bridge. What remains of Wakefield Green will shortly come into view on the left-hand side of the road. Although much of the area is now surrounded by the grey of suburbia, it is nevertheless at this point that the first physical clue to the battlefield appears.

If one looks closely at the boundary wall of the school on the right of Manygates Lane, an iron railing enclosure can be seen, hiding under the umbrella of foliage from the surrounding trees and shrubs. This enclosure marks the spot where Edward IV first erected a memorial to his father's death and inside it can be found a stone monument, erected in 1897 to replace the original cross destroyed during the siege of Sandal Castle in the English Civil War. The Sandal Castle Report of 1966 states:

As a memorial, the duke's son, when he ascended the throne as Edward the 4th, erected a cross on the spot where his father fell. The cross stood on the west side of Cock and Bottle lane, a hundred yards beyond the junction of this lane and the one running between the castle and the river to Milnthorpe. This was

Memorial to the Duke of York, built at a cost of £140 in 1897. It is said to have been built on the spot where Edward IV had ordered a wooden cross to be erected to mark the death of his father. Dr Walker was instrumental in the erection of the monument. The original position of the wooden cross is believed to have been a little further north. (G. Wheeler)

demolished by the Roundheads in the Civil War but another memorial, in the form of a column (now present) was erected at the same place in 1897.[16]

The monument is about 12 feet in height and from a point about 2 feet below its pinnacle it is carved with ornate decorations, some of which have sadly been vandalized. Near its base is an inscription which reads 'Richard Plantagenet Duke of York – fighting for the cause of the white rose fell on this spot in the battle of Wakefield December 30th 1460.' To the right of this is an endorsement by the people who were responsible for the monument's erection, which reads 'This stone is erected in 1897 by some who wish to preserve the traditional site.' Also upon the monument are four decorative panels on which are carved the arms and motto of the Duke of York: the falcon and fetterlock, the white rose, and the broom plant (*planta genista*), the emblem from which the Plantagenets took their name. Although most of the people who caused the monument to be erected are unknown, it is said that Dr J.W. Walker played a fundamental part in its creation and that it cost some £140.

The inscription on the monument claims that this was the spot where the Duke of York made his last stand. However, on page 383 of W.S. Banks's *Walks about Wakefield*, printed in 1871, there is an engraving, said to be taken from a photograph by G. Hall, which shows two willow trees growing on the spot which

Detail of the inscription on the base of memorial. (G. Wheeler)

Detail of the figure of Richard Duke of York from the Victorian monument. It is copied from the original statue (right) which once adorned the Welsh bridge at Shrewsbury, but is now on the Market Hall. (G. Wheeler)

is now the most northerly point, or apex, of the triangular piece of ground on which the school is built. These two willow trees may be the ones mentioned by Brooke, who visited the spot in 1852, by Tyas in 1854 and by Markam in 1886, at which time only one remained – and could be the true location of the duke's death.

The school building and playground are built upon the 'triangular piece of

Detail of the top of the memorial. The inscription to the left of the figure – 'por bon amour' – is taken from the words engraved on a ring which was found on the battlefield. The inscription translates as either 'for good love' or 'in true love'. (G. Wheeler)

ground, with a fence about it' that Mr Norisson Scatcherd alluded to in the extract quoted earlier. Therefore, if this is the site of the duke's last stand, and thus indicates the route of the Yorkists' fighting retreat towards the safety of the castle, then both the park opposite and the school playground behind it were, over five hundred years ago, the scene of desperate slaughter. Richard Knowles's recently published research on the topography of the battlefield indicates that an old medieval road circumnavigated the castle and then followed a course very close to that of today's Milnthorpe Lane, along the western boundary of the triangular piece of ground to a point a little beyond the apex and beyond, approximately to the point where the modern railway bridge crosses Manygates Lane, and joins the northern boundary of Wakefield Green before heading north towards the bridge at Wakefield itself. This is interesting because it adds weight to the argument that the site mentioned above was indeed the location of the duke's last stand, since it is likely that the medieval road would have been the easiest route for the Duke and his men to take during their fighting retreat.

Many people believe that the lane is haunted. It is said that, even in recent years, some locals have commented on 'unusual experiences'. Indeed, a 'very thoroughly Yorkshire warning', has come down to us, which reads: 'Mind th'

The northern point of the triangular piece of ground mentioned by many historians as being the location of the Duke of York's death and the true location of the wooden cross ordered to be erected by Edward IV to mark his father's demise. The road to the left is Manygates Lane and the road to the right follows the same route as the medieval road. It is likely that the Duke of York attempted a fighting retreat back to the castle – located out of sight beyond the brow of the hill – along the route of this road, adding credence to the belief that this area does indeed mark the true location of his death. (Author's collection)

Duke o' York, without his head, doesn't git ho'd o' th', as th' gans by th' willo' tree.'

From here, all that remains is to return to Sandal Castle. Along the way, a little beyond the monument on the right-hand side of the road, just before the end of the triangular piece of ground, is the site of the well that Brooke remarked on. Like the Cock and Bottle public house, the well has long since disappeared. After completing this walk, the walker would surely appreciate – as I am sure Brooke did, after completing his own exploration of the battlefield – the refreshment that either would have afforded.

CHAPTER EIGHT

Conclusions

. . . Like a whirlwind from the north . . .

THE ABSENCE OF GRAVE PITS

The battle of Wakefield is a conundrum in many ways; indeed, even the site of the actual battlefield is uncertain. One of the major problems is the absence of grave pits containing the remains of those who were slain in the battle. It was a great slaughter – so where were they buried? Brooke, who visited the battlefield before twentieth-century development destroyed it for ever, was also at a loss to answer this question. He wrote:

> There has not been discovered, within the memory of man, any large trench or pit near Sandal Church, where it might reasonably be supposed that some of the slain would be interred, such as has been discovered at Battlefield Church, in consequence of the battle of Shrewsbury, and at Saxton Church, in consequence of the battle of Towton.[1]

I can offer no positive solution to this question, other than to suggest that the dead are interred somewhere near Portobello House. The only evidence I have to offer in support of this is the following. The contour lines on the Ordnance Survey map of the 1850s clearly show that Portobello House was situated in a natural dip. It is possible that this natural dip was used to collect together the dead bodies, and that they were buried at that point, in the open ground south of the housing estate, towards the river. It is only here, on the site of Portobello House, that any quantity of remains – in the form of bones, artefact and weapons – are said to have been found. Other than a few weapons and other debris of war discovered in the 'Fall Ings' and east of the Barnsley–Wakefield Road, there is no other evidence to suggest where the two thousand or more troops believed to have died in the battle, are laid to rest.

THE BATTLE OF ST ALBANS

Following the Lancastrians' victory at Wakefield, and their reunion at York with Margaret of Anjou and her army of Scottish/northern mercenaries, the Lancastrian commanders turned their attention to liberating King Henry VI from his Yorkist captors in London. Early in January, they set off with their whole army southwards along the Great North Road. Although the Lancastrian force included many nobles, and they marched under the banner of the Prince of Wales, with his emblems of the white swan and ostrich feather, their army was little more than a disorderly rabble, particularly the northern mercenaries. Their devastating march south is well chronicled,[2] and it appears that the Lancastrian commanders – who were short of funds – allowed the mercenaries a free hand as they moved south. Numerous Yorkist towns south of the River Trent were savagely plundered, emphasizing the predominantly north–south conflict. The towns with Yorkist sympathies were hardest hit, including Stamford, Grantham, Peterborough, Huntingdon and Royston; they were seen by the Lancastrian command as fair game, not only to help victual the army in the mid-winter months, but also to pay the Scottish mercenaries – in the absence of Lancastrian money – for their services.

This did much to rouse hatred of the Lancastrians, a fact that the Yorkists were able to use to their advantage in rallying the common folk to their cause, as shown by the following lines from the contemporary ballad, 'The Rose of Rouen', taken from *Archaeologia*, vol. XXIX, 1842, p. 344:

> . . . All the lords of the north they wrought by one assent,
> for to destroy the south country they did entent,
> had not the Rose of Rouen [Edward IV] been,
> all England had been shent . . .

This permission to pillage severely damaged what little favourable public opinion the Lancastrians held with the population south of the River Trent, and brought massive destruction to many of the pro-Yorkist towns along the Great North Road, as the Lancastrian army slowly approached London. The Prior of Croyland Abbey described the destruction as follows:

> The duke [of York] being thus removed from this world, the northemen, being sensible that [the] only impediment was now withdrawn, and that there was no one now who would care to resist their inroads, again swept onwards like a whirlwind from the north, and in the impulse of their fury attempted to overrun the whole of England . . .
>
> . . . Thus did they proceed with inpunity, spreading in vast multitudes over a space of thirty miles in bredth [across the Great North Road] and, covering the whole surface of the earth just like a plague of Locusts, made their way almost to the very walls of London; all the moveables which they could possibly collect in every quarter placed on beasts of burden and carried off. With such avidity for spoil they did press on, that they dug up precious vessels which, through fear of them, had been concealed in the earth, and with threats of death compelled the people to produce the treasures which they had hidden in remote and obscure spots.
>
> What do you suppose must have been our fears dwelling here in this island, when every day rumours of this sad nature were reaching our ears, and we were

in the utmost dread that we should have to experience similar hardships to those which had been inflicted by them upon our neighbours . . .[3]

Meanwhile the Earl of Warwick, apparently aware of the disaster which had befallen the Yorkists at Wakefield, and despite the sorrow of losing not only his father, but also his brother, uncle and cousin, began mustering his forces in London ready to repel the northern hordes that his scouts had informed him were approaching the capital. The ranks of the Yorkist army were swelled by many men who had either fled from, or heard about, the destruction inflicted by Margaret's northern army and who now sought the protection of the one man whom they felt could save them – the Earl of Warwick. On 12 February the Yorkist army left the city and marched northwards, ready to face the Lancastrians in battle.

At the same time, many of the citizens who had remained in London began to bury their possessions and secure their premises, as the above quote shows, and a grim atmosphere of fear settled over the city. The people nervously awaited the outcome of the battle, greatly fearful of the consequences for their city if Warwick should lose.

When his forces reached St Albans, the Earl of Warwick, unable to guess exactly where the Lancastrians would strike, set up a defensive perimeter around the town and waited for the arrival of Margaret's army. Battle was joined at St Albans on 17 February, as the Lancastrians launched themselves at the Yorkist defences.[4] They 'rolled up' the Yorkists' left flank, positioned around St Albans, and totally routed the remaining Yorkists. The Earl of Warwick and several other Yorkist commanders managed to escape but Henry VI, whom Warwick had brought as a hostage from London, was left behind in the panic, and soon found himself reunited with his wife and child.

THE ACCESSION OF EDWARD IV AND THE BATTLE OF TOWTON

The Earl of Warwick retreated with the remnants of his army into the Cotswolds where he was reunited with Edward, Earl of March, and now Duke of York, and his army. Edward, having heard about his father's defeat and death at Wakefield, was marching east to come to the aid of the Earl of Warwick. On 2 or 3 February Edward's troops had met and defeated a Lancastrian force consisting mainly of Welshmen at Mortimers Cross, thus proving himself an able battle commander and raising Yorkist morale. Now realizing that the road to London was open to the Lancastrians, Edward and Warwick decided to march towards the capital.

The Lancastrians, meanwhile, were losing control of their mercenaries. Unable to take full advantage of the Yorkist defeat after the battle of St Albans, Margaret decided that instead of marching on London, they should return to the Lancastrian heartlands in the north. Her decision to return to the north was to prove another turning-point for the Yorkists, whose fortunes in the previous twelve months had swung like a weathercock from their lowest point – the flight from Ludford Bridge – to their highest – their return from exile and the capture of Henry VI at Northampton. The disaster at Wakefield ushered in another low

Edward IV. Portrait c. 1516–22. (Society of Antiquaries, London)

The Great Seal of Edward IV. (G. Wheeler)

for the Yorkists; not only had they lost their figurehead, the Duke of York, but they had been defeated in two major military engagements, in which several of their key military advisers were killed; moreover they had lost control of the king. The only hope was offered by Edward's victory at Mortimers Cross.

However, this situation was to change dramatically when the Yorkists entered the capital on 26 February. It was at this point that the Londoners, elated at their 'reprieve' from disaster at the hands of the Lancastrians, were asked to accept Edward as their king. Edward, who was young, dynamic and certainly more popular than his late father, was certainly a more suitable candidate for the crown than Henry – and the Londoners readily agreed. From that day on, Edward was known as Edward IV, King of England. The following chronicle[5] describes his accession to the throne:

And upon the Thursday following th'Earls of March and of Warwick with a great power of men, entered the city of London, the which of the citizens joyously received, and upon the Sunday following the said earl caused to be mustered his people in St John's Field, where unto that host were proclaimed and shewed certain articles and points that King Henry had offended in, whereupon it was demanded of the said people whether the said Henry were worthy to reign as king any longer or no. Whereupon the people cried hugely and said, Nay, Nay. And after it was asked of them whether they would have th'Earl of March for their king and they cried with one voice, Yea, Yea. After the which admission thus by the commons assented, certain captains were assigned to bear report thereof unto the said Earl of March, then being lodged at his place called Baynard's Castle. Of the which when he was by them ascertained he thanked God and them . . .[6]

Despite this resounding success, Edward knew he still had to deal with the Lancastrian army in the north, and he was well aware that he would have to fight for his crown.

The morale of the Lancastrian army was exceptionally high at this point. With the rescue of the king and two victories behind them, and the death of the Duke of York also to their credit, who could blame them. Clearly, the Lancastrian strategy had changed, as Goodman suggests in his work *The Wars of the Roses*, where he writes:

The Wakefield campaign reveals a new style of military leadership among the Yorkists' opponents – devious, inventive and quick to exploit opportunities. The complacency shown by York and Salisbury over Christmas may have stemmed partly from a failure to grasp that they were dealing with opponents no longer prepared to keep faith with them . . .

. . . The Lancastrians had, indeed, recently lost some of their most experienced and forceful captains (Buckingham, Shrewsbury, Beaumont and Egremont); and two of their present commanders, Somerset and Exeter, had recently failed dismally. The quality of the northern command was again demonstrated after Wakefield in their ability and determination to launch an invasion of the south in mid-winter, culminating in a second victory only seven weeks after the first . . .[7]

Edward IV was all too aware of this, and it can have been rarely far from his mind as the Yorkists began assembling their forces in preparation for their march north to confront the Lancastrians. Edward's intention was to settle the dynastic issue once and for all, and unlike his father, he was well prepared for the conflict to come. As A.W. Boardman wrote:

The war between north and south was to continue, but with a new slant in the form of a man who was prepared, with the help of his followers, to usurp the English throne. Unlike his father, Richard Duke of York, Edward was no longer prepared to keep faith with his enemies – his father's killers – or the king. However, he saw the means, with Warwick's political prowess, if not his military ability, to assert his own character on the Londoners in the guise of a medieval saviour, now that they were desperate for deliverance. He was not only about to bring his father's claims back to life, but also to surpass them, fighting the bloodiest battle on British soil in the process.[8]

The first elements of the Yorkist army left London on 11 March 1461, and Edward himself left two days later, on the 13th. After a march of eighteen days, followed by a preliminary skirmish between themselves and Lord Clifford's men on 28 March at Ferrybridge, the Yorkists finally confronted the Lancastrians at Towton in Yorkshire. Here the two armies – said to number more than 80,000 men – fought a savage battle on Palm Sunday, 29 March 1461. It ended in a resounding victory for the Yorkists, and the Lancastrians were totally routed. Although the Wars of the Roses dragged on for a number of years afterwards, the Lancastrians never really recovered from their defeat at Towton.[9]

When Edward IV entered the city of York after his victory at Towton, he immediately ordered the heads of those who had died at Wakefield to be removed from the gates and walls of the city. They were replaced with the heads of the Lancastrians who had fallen at Towton – or who had been captured and executed after the battle.

THE BURIAL OF THE DUKE OF YORK

The Duke of York, whose death at the age of 49 at Wakefield was the most significant consequence of that battle, was not afforded a funeral appropriate to his rank until 1476, sixteen years later.[10] After Towton, Edward's first priority was to pursue the surviving Lancastrians into Northumberland. Although the remains of the Yorkists were removed from the city walls of York, the heads of Richard, Duke of York, and Edmund, Earl of Rutland, were simply taken to St Richard's Friary[11] in Pontefract where they were hastily interred with their bodies. Their state funerals were planned to take place at a later date, when there were less demanding issues to deal with. It seems likely, therefore, that the mutilation of their bodies had occurred at Pontefract and not at Sandal, as it is unlikely that two headless corpses would have been taken all the way to Pontefract for burial after this barbarous act had been committed.

Once Edward had established peace in his realm, the Duke's body was exhumed from its temporary grave on 20 or 21 July 1476, and taken to its final resting place at the family home of Fotheringhay. The funeral cortege made slow and stately progress. On Sunday 21 July it remained at Pontefract, where prayers were said all day in memory of the Duke of York and the Earl of Rutland. Then the progress began, travelling in short stages, passing through Doncaster, Blyth, Tuxford, Newark and Grantham to Stamford, where it remained during Sunday 28 July, and where again, there was a day of prayer. The journey finished on Monday 29th, when the cortege arrived at Fotheringhay early in the afternoon.

The coffins were carried to Fotheringhay in a specially commissioned hearse, which cost £75 17s 2d, and was built by one John Talbot of London. Planning the journey was a major logistical achievement. At the end of each day, suitable resting places had to be found for the coffins. Equally, nobles who lived along the route had to be informed of the route that the funeral party would be taking, so that they and their households could come to pay their respects. The funeral party itself was escorted from Pontefract by many of the leading nobles of the realm (including some whose ancestors had been involved in York's death). They included Henry Percy, Earl of Northumberland; Thomas, Lord Stanley; Richard Hastings, Lord Welles; Ralph, Lord Greystoke; Humphrey, Lord Dacre; and

Fotheringhay Church, Northants. The sixteenth-century memorial to Richard, Duke of York, Cecily Neville and Edmund, Earl of Rutland, their son, was erected by order of Queen Elizabeth I in 1573. (G. Wheeler)

The remains of the effigies of Richard Neville, Earl of Salisbury, and his wife Alice Montague, Burghfield, Berks. Originally buried in the family mausoleum at Bisham Abbey, they were removed during the dissolution of the monasteries by Henry VIII. (G. Wheeler)

John Blount, Lord Mountjoy. The young Richard, Duke of Gloucester, the late Duke of York's third surviving son and later Richard III, walked solemnly before the funeral cortege all the way to Fotheringhay, where Edward IV soberly awaited their arrival with an even more impressive gathering of nobles, including his brother George, Duke of Clarence; John de la Pole, Earl of Lincoln; Henry Bourchier, Earl of Essex; Edmund Grey, Earl of Kent; Anthony Woodville, Earl Rivers; William, Lord Hastings; Walter Devereux, Lord Ferrers; James Touchet, Lord Audley; and many more.

The funeral took place on Tuesday 30 July and the feasts were attended by over two thousand people. Contemporary and near-contemporary accounts of the funeral are few and far between. Leland wrote that Edward: '. . . caused the body of his father to be brought from Pontefract thither [Fotheringhay] and layid to rest on the north side of the Highe Altare . . .'. The Duchess of York, having outlived all her children bar one, died at Berkhamsted on 31 May 1495, thirty years after her husband, and was buried alongside him at Fotheringhay. Leland

Modern Wakefield has few reminders of the battle. In the 1960s, this title mural, based on a Radio Times *cover design by artist Eric Fraser, was installed in a local hotel. (G. Wheeler).*

described her tomb thus: 'where is also buried, King Edward IV's mother, in a vaulte, over the which is a pratie chappelle'.[12]

After the battle of Wakefield, the Neville family also took pains to mourn the loss of the Earl of Salisbury and his son Sir Thomas Neville; with equal solemnity their bodies were laid to rest at Bisham Abbey in Buckinghamshire, on 15 January 1463. The funeral was attended by all the Neville adherents, the House of York being represented by George, Duke of Clarence, and Elizabeth, Duchess of Suffolk.

FINAL ANALYSIS

It could perhaps be argued that if the battle of Wakefield had not been fought, and the Duke of York had survived, then the Lancastrians' ultimate defeat would not have come to pass. In effect, their destruction was brought about largely through their own actions, the depredations of their march south providing more support for the Yorkist cause than anything the Yorkists could have done, and enabling Edward to take the throne with much popular support. In turn, this allowed the Yorkists to muster a large enough army to destroy the Lancastrians at the battle of Towton. Perhaps if the Lancastrians had employed more acceptable tactics, they might have averted their unpopularity in the south, and their downfall – and the reign of Edward IV – would never have happened. Lack of popular support had meant that Edward's father, Richard, Duke of York, was unlikely to be successful in his claim to the throne, and thus the Lancastrian Henry VI would have remained unchallenged on the throne, and the rest of the Wars of the Roses might not have taken place. Indeed, it is possible that the Yorkist cause could have petered out long before Henry VI died, and even the 'right' of the House of York to ascend to the throne under the Act of Accord of 1460 would have faded away.

Bearing all this in mind, one could say that the outcome of the battle of Wakefield was, in effect, more of a disaster for the Lancastrians than for the Yorkists. Although the Lancastrians won at Wakefield, and again at St Albans a few weeks later, their plundering of the towns on their infamous march south aroused much hatred against them, allowing the Yorkists, whose popularity was much greater under Edward than it ever had been under his father, to assemble a large army and utterly destroy the Lancastrians at the battle of Towton, three months later.

Unfortunately for modern historians, the overwhelming defeat of the Yorkists at Wakefield, combined with the subsequent destruction of the victors of Wakefield at Towton only three months later, left very few witnesses alive to tell the tale of what really happened at Wakefield. This lack of first-hand evidence, combined with the less-than-factual and often 'biased' nature of contemporary chronicles, means that there is precious little credible evidence from which modern historians can piece together the story of the campaign and battle of Wakefield. This means that we are faced with a number of unanswered questions, chief among which are the following:

1. Where did the Yorkists billet their men?
2. Where was the battle actually fought?
3. Did the Lancastrians arrive before the castle on the day of the battle or earlier?
4. Did the Lancastrians prepare a trap?
5. Did the Lancastrians dress their men in the livery of the Earl of Warwick?
6. Why did the Duke of York offer battle?
7. Did the Duke of York die on the field of battle or afterwards?
8. Was the Earl of Rutland murdered at Lord Clifford's hand?
9. Was Queen Margaret present at the battle?
10. Where are the bodies of the slain buried?

Some people might ask whether any of this actually matters. Yet to those of us who wish to understand the battle more fully, this lack of information is hugely frustrating, but it must be added that it is not a problem unique to Wakefield. In this book I have attempted to give credible answers to all the questions listed above, or at the very least, I have put forward a number of theories. It may be frustrating, but perhaps not knowing the whole truth is part of the mystique which makes the battlefields of the Wars of the Roses so interesting to research in the first place.

APPENDIX I

Topography of the Battlefield

In terms of the topography of Wakefield and the area immediately surrounding the battlefield, there are two main elements to consider with respect to the battle of Wakefield. The first is the near-contemporary quote that the battle was fought 'in the plain ground between his castle and the town of Wakefield'; at first glance, this seems to suggest open grassland, reminiscent of today's 'plains'. According to Richard Knowles, who wrote extensively on the subject, the medieval open fields were at the time of the battle certainly under plough cultivation: indeed, the remains of ridge and furrow still survive to a limited extent on what remains of Sandal Common (today known as Wakefield Green). The open fields were probably divided by thick stock-proof hedges, often with drainage ditches next to them. These would have proved very difficult for any troops to cross.

One of the medieval open fields was called Castlefield and this name survived for several centuries. One of the earliest references to it occurs in a previously unpublished deed of 1415, which also confirms the existence of drains and ditches. The name also appears on the Sandal Enclosure Map of 1800 (see Figure D), some four hundred years later. It seems reasonable to conclude that if the Castlefield was present and under cultivation in 1415, then by 1460 even greater areas of land would have been brought under the plough as the population grew.

The second point under consideration here forms a major component in any study of the conflict, especially with regard to the accepted account of the battle – the issue of the presence or otherwise of dense wooded areas (known as 'parkes'), immediately to the east and west of the castle. Sandal Park constituted the only substantial wooded area in the immediate proximity of the castle and, according to the rent roll of 1545–6: 'the parke adionyng conteyneth by estimation XL acres well paled wherein are XXX fallowe deere or therabouts'.[1] As Knowles points out, 'An army would not have been able to march with any ease through a paled wood.' He continued:

> . . . This [Sandal Park] would have presented a formidable obstacle around the castle, although it was obviously not large enough to have supplied sufficient meat for the garrison during the busy Christmas of 1460. The foraging parties

Wakefield Green looking north-east. Clearly shown in this photograph are the remains of medieval 'ridge and furrow', indicating the farming methods which were prominent in the area of the battlefield at the time of the conflict. (Author's collection)

referred to in the near contemporary accounts may have been into the town of Wakefield, or more likely to one of the parks on the north bank of the Calder, either the 'olde parke' or the 'new parke', both of which are recorded in a survey of 1564. The new park in particular is said to have been 'well replenished with deare to the numbers of three hundreth'. These parks complete with pales are clearly shown on the John Speed map of the West Riding dated 1610.[2]

There is no doubt that there was a wood near the castle, but in the absence of a detailed map of the area dating from that time, we have no evidence for its precise location or size. It is therefore impossible to say whether an armed force, as detailed in the 'accepted' account of the battle (*see* Chapter Five), could have been bivouacked in the wood, concealed from the occupants of the castle. On John Speed's map,[3] Sandal Park can clearly be seen to the west of Sandal village and south of the River Calder. The park is shown surrounding the castle but does not extend as far north as the banks of the river. Sadly, however, the scale of the map does not offer us any further clues as to its extent.

In conclusion, we are unable to quantify in detail the exact location and density

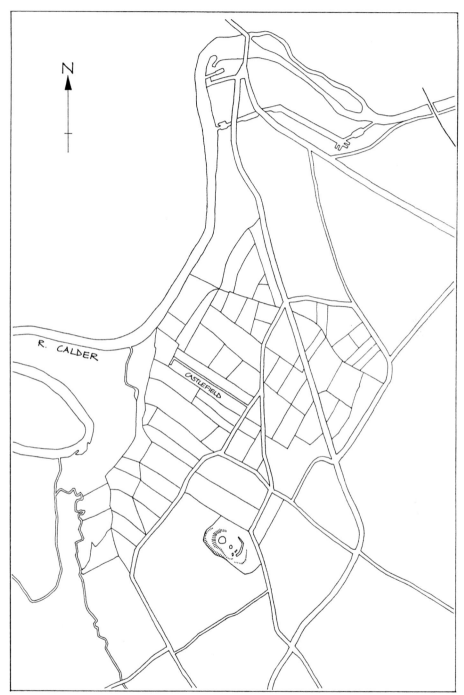

Figure D: this drawing, taken from the Enclosure map dated 1800, shows the position of 'Castlefield'.

of the woods around Sandal at the time of the battle. It is impossible to know how close the woods were to the castle itself, although defensive requirements would have prevented the wood encroaching too near. It does seem likely that the wooded areas extended to the south, west and east of the castle, but cleared to the north, towards the river.

Author's note: In light of this information regarding the wooded area known as Sandal Park and its relation to Sandal Castle, I feel obliged to point out that on the maps in this book the extent of the wooded areas is not based on fact, but on conjecture, taking into account the available evidence.

APPENDIX II

The Chroniclers and their Chronicles

If we are to understand fully all the facts surrounding the battle of Wakefield, we should consider the work of the chroniclers of the time, both contemporary and otherwise. Clements Markham, in his paper on the battle of Wakefield, mentioned the chronicles and gave a summary of the life of the chroniclers. As I have quoted from Markham in this work, it seems fitting to include his words regarding the chroniclers. What follows is therefore a resumé of Markham's work together with the text of the chronicles relevant to the campaign and the battle of Wakefield.

However, where Markham has made no comment, I have written a short passage regarding that particular chronicler. I would like to point out that Markham wrote his work late in the last century, and since that time research regarding the chroniclers has continued and new information has come to light.[1]

For example, K.B. McFarlane has proved conclusively that William of Worcester did not write *Annales*. In modern works references to *Annales* is now credited to either 'Anonymous' or as 'Pseudo–Worcester'. In this work, owing to the large number of works that are quoted within it, where *Annales* is credited to Worcester, then in order to avoid confusion between my work and quoted material, as regards the chroniclers, I have done the same.

WILLIAM OF WORCESTER

William of Worcester was the son of a person of the same name who lived at St James Bee, in the town of Bristol, and was descended on his mother's side from a family of Coventry named Botoner. He sometimes signed himself William Botoner, but is better known as William of Worcester.

This writer has special advantage as a reliable narrator of contemporary events. Born in 1415, he entered the University of Oxford in 1432. He was secretary to Sir John Fastolf, and was for many years steward of his manor of Castle Combe in Wiltshire . . . He was about 45 years of age in 1460, and was in London at the time of the accession of Edward IV. His work *Annales* was first published by Thomas Hearne in 1771.

His account is as follows:

> Parliament being prorogued in December, the duke and earl [York and Salisbury] hastened from London with a large armed force towards York, but coming unexpectedly upon the troops of the Duke of Somerset at Worksop, their vanguard was destroyed. On the 21st of December, however, they reached Sandal Castle, with 6,000 men. The duke came to the castle of Sandal besides Wakefield on Christmas Eve, and there began to assemble his tenants and friends.
>
> The followers of the Duke of York, having gone out to forage for provisions on the 29th of December, a dreadful battle was fought at Wakefield between the Duke of Somerset, the Earl of Northumberland and Lord Neville, and the adverse party, when the Duke of York, Thomas Neville, son of the Earl of Salisbury, Thomas Harrington, Thomas Parr, Edward Bourchier, James Pykering, and Henry Rathforde, with many other Knights and Squires, and soldiers to the amount of two thousand, were slain in the field.
>
> After the battle, Lord Clifford slew the young Earl of Rutland, the son of the Duke of York, as he was fleeing across the Bridge at Wakefield; and in the same night the Earl of Salisbury was captured by a follower of Sir Andrew Trollope, and on the morrow beheaded by the Bastard of Exeter at Pontefract, where at the same time the dead bodies of York Rutland, and others of note who fell in the battle, were decapitated, and their heads affixed in various parts of York, whilst a paper crown was placed in derision on the head of the Duke of York.

Annales Rerum Angelicarum (In *Exchequer Liber Niger Scaccarii Nec Non Wilhelmi Worcestrii*), vol. II, pp. 484–5. Translation taken from *The Chronicles of the White Rose of York*, LXXXIII, ed. J.C. Giles, 1843.

There is another account of the actual battle credited to Worcester, which appears in *Annales Rerum Angelicarum*, vol. II, p. 775, ed. J. Stevenson, 1884. It is as follows:

> On 21st December the Duke of York and the Earl of Salisbury, with 6,000 soldiers came to Sandal Castle, where they spent Christmas, the Duke of Somerset and the Earl of Northumberland with the opposite party lying meanwhile at Pontefract, King Henry with the Earl of Warwick and others spent Christmas in the Palace of the Bishop of London at St Paul's. Edward Earl of March spent Christmas in the town of Shrewsbury at the Friary. On December 29th at Wakefield, when the Duke of York's men were roaming through the countryside for victuals, a horrible battle was fought between them and the Duke of Somerset, the Earl of Northumberland and Lord Neville with a great army; and there were killed in the field the Duke of York, Thomas Neville, son of the Earl of Salisbury, Thomas Harrington . . . many other knights and squires, and common soldiers to the number of 2,000. And after the battle Lord Clifford killed Lord Edmund, Earl of Rutland son of the Duke of York, on the bridge at Wakefield as he fled. And the same night the Earl of

Salisbury was captured by a servant of Andrew Trollope. And on the morrow at Pontefract the Bastard of Exeter killed the Earl of Salisbury, and there by the counsel of the lords they beheaded the bodies of the Duke of York, the Earls of Salisbury and Rutland . . . and placed their heads on various gateways of York. The head of the Duke of York they also in contempt crowned with a paper crown.

WILLIAM GREGORY

His account is as follows:

Then the queen having knowledge of this party while she sent unto the Duke of Somerset, at that time being in Dorsetshire at the castle of Corfe, and for the Earl of Devonshire, and for Alexander Hody, and prayed them to come to her hastily as they might, with their tenants as strong in their harness to war, for the Lord Roos, the Lord Clifford, the Baron of Greystock, the Lord Neville, the Lord Latimer, were waiting upon the Duke of Exeter to meet with her in Hull. And this matter was not tarried but full privily i-wrought; and she sent letters unto all her chief officers that they would do the same, and that they should warn all who servants that loved her or purposed to keep or rejoice their office, to wait upon her at Hull by that day as it appointed by her. All these people gathered and conveyed so privily that they were whole in number of 15,000 ere any man would believe it; in so much if any man said, or told, or talked of such gathering, he should be schende [disgraced] and some were in great danger, for the common people said by thoo that told the truth, 'Ye talk right ye would it were', and given no credence of their saying. But last the lords proposed to know the truth.

. . . And the 9th day of December next following set out the Duke of York, the Earl of Salisbury, the Earl of Rutland and Sir Thomas Harrington, with many more knights and squires and great people with them, and so departed out of London towards York.

Gregory's Chronicle, pp. 208–10 in *The Historical Collections of a Citizen of London*, ed. J. Gairdner (Camden Society, 1876).

JOHN LELAND

John Leland should not really be considered a contemporary chronicler, as he was commissioned by Henry VIII to complete an itinerary of England, and in the process visited Yorkshire in 1558. The following text from his works is rather a list than a chronicle of what he saw at the town of Wakefield. However, he does tell us a little about the battle and he no doubt received his information from the people he met when he came to the town. His account is as follows:

These thinges I especially notid in Wakefield.
    The faire Bridge of Stone of 9 Arches, under the which reunith the Ryver of

Calder. And on the Est side of this Bridge is a right goodly Chapel of our Lady and 2 Cantuarie Prestes foundid in it, of the fundation of the Townes Men as sum say: but the Dukes of York were taken as founders for obteyning the Mortemayn.

I Heard one say that a servant of King Edwardes (the 4) father, or els of the Erle of Rutheland, brother to King Edwarde the 4 was a great doer of it.

There was a sore Batell faught in the south Feeldes by this Bridge. And yn the flite of the Duke of Yorkes Parte, other the duke hymself, or his Sun therle of Rutheland, was slayne a little above the barres beyond the Bridge going up into the Toune of Wakefield that standith ful fairely apon a clyving ground. At this place is set up a Crosse in rei memoriam.

The commune saying is there, that the Erle wold have taken ther a poore Woman's House for socour, and she for fere shet the Dore and strait the Erle was killid. The Lord Clifford for killing of Men at this Batail was caullid the Boucher . . . '

Itinerary, vol. I, fo. 44–5 (1558 – The Yorkshire extracts, as shown in the *Yorkshire Archaeological Journal*, vol. 10. (1889), pp. 241–2).

ROLLS OF PARLIAMENT

The Rolls of Parliament contain a number of relevant facts regarding the campaign and battle of Wakefield. The printed version of the Rolls of Parliament is available in six volumes titled *Rotuli Parliamentorum*, first produced in 1767. A number of extracts from this work follow, which refer to various aspects of the Wakefield Campaign. (The Act of Attainder is printed in full as Appendix IV.)

ON THE ACT OF ACCORD:

There are a number of aspects regarding the Act of Accord mentioned in the Rolls of Parliament. The events leading up to the act begin on page 375 of *Rotuli Parliamentorum*. Firstly, the Duke of York's claim to the crown is explored, and it is written that on:

> . . . the XVI day of Octobr, the IXth daye of this prefent Parlement, the Counfeill of the right high and myghty Prynce Richard Duc of York, brought into the Parlement Chambre a writyng, conteignyng the clayme and title of the right, that the feid Duc pretended unto the Crones of Englond and Fraunce, and Lordship of Irelond . . .

This was followed by an account of York's pedigree and title. The following day (17 October, the X day of Parliament) York again entered Parliament and asked what was to be done regarding his claim. The Lords in response stated that:

> . . . the mater was fo high and of fuch wyght, that it was not to eny of the

Kynges Subgetts to enter into communication therof . . . it was thought and agreed by all the Lordes, that they all fhuld goo unto the Kyng, to declare and open the feid mater unto his Higness, and to underftond what his good grace wuld to be doon ferther therin . . .

The issue having been presented to the king (on 18 July, the XI day of Parliament) Henry deferred the issue to his Justices, and asked them to 'advise and council on his behalf'. The Justices, having considered the issue (on 20 July, the XIII day of Parliament) came to the Lords and claimed that the issue was:

. . . so high, and touched the Kyngs high eftate and regalie, which is above the lawe and paffed ther lernyhg, wherfore they durft not enter into any communication therof . . .

Therefore, the Lords raised the issue to the 'Kyngs Sergeauntes and Attourney, and gave theym ftraight commaundment in the Kyngs name'.

On 22 July, the XV day of Parliament, they stated certain objections to York's claim, amongst which, was the following, that:

. . . the Lordes of this lond muft nedes calle to their remembrauncez, the grete Othes the which they have mede to the Kyng oure Soverayn Lord, the which may be leyde to the feid Duc of York, and that the Lordes may not breke thoo Othes . . . it is thought yf the seid Duc fhuld make eny title or clayme, by the lyne of Sir Leonell, that the same Duc fhuld bere the armes of the fame Leonell, and not the armes of Edmund Langley late Duc of York.

This was followed by York's response, as stated in the Rolls:

To the which Articles the feid Duc of York yave his anfwers in writing as folowen:

Firstly, regarding his previous oath to serve Henry VI:

Furft, where it is faid that it is thought that the Lordes of this lond muft nedes calle to their remembrauncez, the grete Othes the which they have mede to the Kyng, which may be leyde to the feid Duc, and that they may not breke thoo Othes.
   The faid Richard anfwereth and faith, that every man, under peyne of everlaftyng dampnation, is bounden to obeye to the lawe and commaundementes of God, by the which lawe and commaundementes, trouth and juftice owe to be perferred and obferved, and untrouth that of this bonde and duetee of Obedyence to Godds lawe, noo man may discharge hymfilf by his owen dede or act, promiffe or ooth, for elles of the contrary wold enfue innumerable inconveniences. Wherefore fith it is foo, that the mater of the title and clayme of the feid Richard Plantaginet, is openly true and lawfull, and grounded upon evident trouth and juftice, it foloweth that man fhuld have rather confideration to trouth, right and justice in this mater accordyngly with

the will of the lawe of God, then to any promife or ooth made by hym into the contrarie; confidered namely, that by the lawe and determination of holy Chirche, an oth made by oon perfone, unto the the prejudice or hurt of an other, contrary to trouth, justice and charitiee, in the which ftandeth the plenitude and perfection of Godds lawe, is voide and noon effect . . .

Secondly, regarding his lineage and pedigree:

The feid Duc anfwereth and faith, that trouth is, that he myght lawfully have born the armes of the faid Sr Leonell herebifore, and alfo the fame armes that Kyng Edward the third bare, that is to fay, the armes of the Realmes of Englond and of Fraunce; but he abfteyned of beryng of the feid armes, lyke as he abfteigned for the tyme, of purpofyng and purfuyng of his right and title &c. for caufes not unknown to all this Reaume; for though right for a tyme reft and be put to filence, yit it roteth not ner fhall not perifh.

ITEM, where it is allegged ayenft the title of the faid Duc, that the faid Herry of Derby, at fuch tyme as he toke the fame Corone of Englond, and that he entred and toke the fame Corone upon hym, as right enheriter to Kyng Herry the third, and not as a Conquerour.

The feid Duc therto faith, that fuch faying of the fied Kyng Herry the fourth, may in noo wife be true, and that the contray therof, which is trouth, fhall be largely ynough fhewed, approved and juftified, by fufficiant auctorite and matre of record. And over that, that his fied faying was oonly to fhadowe and colour fraudulently his faid unrightwife and violent ufurpation, and by moyen to abufe difceyvably the people ftondyng about hym.

Having answered the questions asked of him, the Lords then delivered their findings and claimed that King Henry would remain 'Kyng of Englond and of Fraunce and Lord of Irelond . . . duryng his lyf naturall', after which the Duke of York would 'bee entitled, called and reputed from hens forth, verrey and rightfull heire to the Corones, Roiall Eftates, Dignite and Lordfhip abovefaid'. But there were conditions: 'and for that tyme, the faid Duc withoute hurte or prejudice of his faid right and title, fhall take, wurfhip and honour hyn for his Soverayn Lord'.

Thus, the duke, having been declared Heir Apparent, took the following oaths:

I Richard Duc of York, promitte and fwere by the feith and trouth that I owe to Almyghty God, that I fhall never doo, confente, procure or ftirre, directely or indirectely, in prive or appert, ner afmuch as in me is and fhall bee, fuffre to bee doo, confented, procure or ftirred, any thing that may bee or fowne to the abriggement of the naturall lyf of Kyng Henry the fixt . . .

His sons took the same oaths, as stated in the Rolls of Parliament: 'Edmund Erle of Marche, and Edmund Erle of Ruthlond, the fonnes of the feid Richard Duc of York, fhall make lyke Ooth.'

Rot. Par. 39, Henry VI (1460), vol. V, pp. 375–80.

ON THE RAVAGING OF THE NORTHERN ESTATES AND LANDS BY THE PERCY FAMILY:

Forsomoche as Thomas Percy Knyght Lord Egremond, and Richard Percy Squier, Brothre to the faid Lord, diverfez and many tymes have raifede, affemblede and gadrede, your people of the Shires of York, Cumb', Weftmerland and Northumberlande, in grete nombre togidre, and daily draw unto them grete nombre of people grete mifdoers, with many othre idle Men of grete riotous rule and mifgovernance, and grete affrayes and riottes have hayneoufly committed within the faid Shires, and many wrongfull entrees as wele forcibly and otherwife have made, for mayntenance of othre mens quarrelles, in Lands, Tenemis and Poffeffions, of diverfes your true and wele ruled liege people of the fame Shires, ayeinft your Paix and Lawes, as it is fuppofed: Wherof your people of the same Shires have been, and yit bee, fore hurt, vexed and troubled, and dare noon entre make, ne Action attempt upon ne ayenft hem at Lawe, for fere of Deth, to her likely deftruction . . . '

Rot. Par. 39, Henry VI (1460), vol. V, pp. 394–5.

ON THE DECISION TO MARCH NORTH TO SUPPRESS THE LANCASTRIAN FORCES:

The King, underftandyng and heryng of the grete rebellions, murdres; riottes, unlawfull and felenoufe fpulyng of his fubgetts, haynous extorfions and oppreffions, daily ufed, attempted and committed, in dyvers parties of his reaume of Englond and Wales, ayenft the good publique and common wele therof; wherof is nat unlyke to growe and enfue, nat oonly the fubverfion of the good and reftfull governaunce of the fais Realme, but alf the outrageous and ymmefurable perturbation and violence of the peas ans tranquillite therof; wherof to daungeroufe and to perilous courage mowe be put in the hertis and myndes of his Enemyes and Adverfaries of Scotland and Fraunce, to avaunce and halt hem into th'execution of their indurat and infaciat malice, purofed and ymagined uppon his feid Reaume, and his fubgettz therof, which in late dayes have born and fuffred, and daily bere and fuffre, to grete, to lamentable, and to grevous affaultes and hurtes of the faid Enemyes; hath, by th'avis of the Lordes Spirituelx and Temporelx, and Commens, in this prefent Parlement affembled, and by auctorite therof, ordeyned and ftablished, that his derreft Coufyn Richard, vray and rightfull heire of the Reaumes of Englond and Fraunce, and of the Lordship and Land of Ireland, Duc of York, have and take uppon hym the charge and labour, to ride into the parties of the feid Realme of England and Wales, where the feid rebellions, murdres, riottes, fpoilyng, extorfions and oppreffions, be ufed, committed ans attempted, to repreffe, fubdue and appefe them, and also to fefift his feid Enemyes of Fraunce and Scotland within his feid Realme; wherunto is neceffarily required th'attendaunce of the faid fubgetts; and therfore graunteth, ordeyneth and ftabliffeth, by the feid advis and auctorite, that every Shirref, with the power and myght of his shirwyk, and every Maire, Baillyf, Officer, Minifter and Subgett, of his feid Realme of Englond and Wales, fhall attend upon his feid Coufyn for the faid entent, as the cas fhall require, and to the fame entent be redy at the commaundement of his faid Coufyn, and the fame obeye and perfourme, in lyke cas as they aught to doo to his commaundment, after the cours of the laws of Englond, and in Wales after the cuftumes there.

And furthermore ordeyneth, graunteth and ftabliffeth, by the feid advis and auctorite, that rebellion, infurrection, disobeifaunce, offence, doon to or ayenft his faid Coufyn, in execution of the feid charge under the Kynges auctorite, or any thyng belongyng therto, by any perfone or perfones, of what eftate or condition foo ever he or they bee, bee taken, demed, reputed, had and accepted, as thing in lyke cas doon to or ayenft his perfone and commaundement.

And furtjhermore ordeyneth, graunteth and ftablisfheth, by the feid advis and auctorite, that his faid Coufyn, at any tyme that he taketh upon hym to ride to the opreffyng of any of the faid rebellions or riottis, fhall have fuch competent, convenient and agreable reward for his coftes and charges, as fhall be thought refonable to the Kyng and his Counfeill, and therof fhall have fure and fufficient paiement . . .

Rot. Par. 39, Henry VI (1460), vol. V, pp. 382–3.

All the above extracts are taken from *Rotuli Parliamentorum* (Record Commission, 1767), vol. V, pp. 374–95.

PASTON LETTERS

The Paston Letters are a collection of letters retained by several members of the prominent fifteenth-century East Anglian Paston family, and preserved through to this day. Members of the Paston family were involved in several of the campaigns and battles of the Wars of the Roses. Indeed, one of them was actually wounded in the battle of Barnet in 1471. They appear to have survived the rise of the Tudors and prospered, despite local rivalry – which resulted in the siege of one of their castles (Caister) – with the Duke of Norfolk. The letters are available in published form in an edition edited by James Gairdner, *The Paston Letters* (Sutton Publishing, 1986).

To John Paston from Clement Paston, 23 January 1461:

Rythe reuerent and worchypfwll broder, recomawnde [me] to you, certyfyng you þat your letter was delyueryd me þe xxiij day of Januari abowthe no o ne seison, and Rychard Calle rode in þe mornyng, and þerefore I brak yowre letter if þere were ony asti mater. And I dede Cristofye Hanswm goo to my Lord of Cawnterburi to tell him as yowre letter rehersyd and my lord seyd he hadde spokyn wyth yowre man þere-of þe day before, and if þe Byssope of Norwyche wold not doo so mwche for him he hijs þe les be-hold to him. Not wythstondyng he sayd he wold saue youharmelez a-yens John yowng; but, and ye do well, remembire thys lordys haue many materijs to thyng on, and if it be fore-getin þe harm is yowrys. And also if þe word torn John yong will not doo at hijs prayere.

And my Lord FitzWatere is rydyn northe-wardys, and it is sayd in my lord of Cawnterberijs howse þat he hathe takyn ij c of Andrew Troloppys men. And as fore Colt and Sire Jamys Strangwysse [Strangways] and Sire Thomas Pykeryng [Pickering], þey be takyn ore ellys dede; þe comyn voysse is þat þey be dede. Hopton and Hastyngys be wyth þ[e] Earle of Marche, and wer not at þe fewlde [Wakefield]. Wat word þat euer he haue from my lordys þat be here, it is well do and best fore yow to see þat þe contre be all-weys redy to com, bothe fote men and hors men, qw a n they be sent fore, fore I have hard seyde þe forthere lordys will be here sonere þan men wen, I haue arde sayde ore iij wekys to an ende . . .

. . . Wrytyn ye xxiij day of janwari in haste, wan I was not well hesse. God haue yow in hijs keping.

By Clement Paston, yowre broder.

The Paston Letters, ed. James Gairdner, vol. 3, ff. 249–50 (Sutton Publishing, 1986).

JEAN DE WAURIN

Originally a soldier (he fought at Agincourt for the English) Jean de Waurin later came to England to serve as a diplomat for the Dukes of Burgundy. He was fascinated by history and recorded what he witnessed in England as well as in Europe. His accounts of the Wars of the Roses are quite informative. However, like Hall, he tended to make up speeches for the people who were present at set encounters, which of course cannot be substantiated. He referred to many contemporary chronicles in completing his own, and extracts from the *Arrivall* and the *Chronicle of the Rebellion in Lincolnshire* appear in his works.

His account is as follows:

> *How the Queen of England, knowing that the king her husband had resigned his crown in favour of the Duke of York and his heirs after his death, asked the Duke of Somerset to take care of the Duke of York.*
>
> After all these agreements done as you heard [the Act of Accord], the Duke of York, and the Earl of March his son, the Earl of Warwick and all the lords there took leave of the king, and soon after they left the royal court, the Earl of March took leave of his father and went to Wales with his people; but the Earl of Salisbury stayed with the Duke of York and so did the Earl of Rutland son of the Duke of York and Sir Thomas Neville son of the Earl [of Salisbury]; they all rode together to a town called Wakefield. When the Duke of York arrived to comply with the king's wish, he gathered 10,000 warriors and they let the queen know that the king wanted her to go to London. When the queen got the news and knowing the decision of the king herein her husband to resign his

crown and his kingdom after his death in favour of the Duke of York and his heirs, she was very troubled because of her love for her only child she had with the king and to see him deprived of his patrimony. Therefore she went defying the Duke of York. The latter hearing the news [that the queen would not consent to such appointment], started to approach the queen, of which she was well informed.

Therefore she sent someone to get the Duke of Somerset to who she asked the place where the Duke of York and his people were staying. The king was informed that the West Country and Cornwall, where the Queen Margaret his wife was in person, was rebelling against the dis-inheritance of her son.

When the young Duke of Somerset heard of the wish of the queen, he gathered a lot of people to fight the Duke of York and his troops. He sought advice of Andrew Trollope who was staying with him, who said he will soon answer him. We will talk later about the Duke of Somerset who had gathered a lot of people to contradict the Duke of York's plans (which he was not really expecting), and will also talk about the named Duke of York.

How the Duke of York and Earl of Salisbury were defeated by the betrayal of Andrew Trollope and a couple of other Lords.

The Duke of York, who was then staying in Wakefield, hearing that the Queen Margaret was coming with the Duke of Somerset and a big group of armed men in order to fight, was as such concerned for at that time he did not have enough people to resist against such a demonstration of force. He talked with the Earl of Salisbury and all the people on his side to review their situation and tried to get people from everywhere in an attempt to increase their strength and power within the town, but all this did not suffice as at that time [the time of the invasion] most of the people were out in the fields

Andrew Trollope, who was a very subtle man of war, told the Duke of Somerset that they would not be able to get the Duke of York outside the town [castle] without consequent human losses. They therefore prepared 400 of the most courageous men, well indoctrinated for what they had to do – i.e. they were to go into the town [castle] and tell the duke that they were coming from Lancashire to rescue him. When the Duke of York, that never suspected such betrayal, saw all those people coming to him, he was so happy that he let them in straight away. That same night the Duke of York organised for somebody to be on the watch in order to make sure that the Duke of Somerset was in the field and observe the extent of his power.

But at the dawn of the day Andrew Trollope accompanied by other warriors, informed the Duke of York, without introducing themselves, that they were coming to rescue him, which made the duke so joyful that he went outside the town [castle] to fight his enemies.

It was then that Andrew Trollope betrayed him, knowing the Duke of Somerset to be nearby, he started the skirmish and the Duke of Somerset who was ready, charged viciously the Duke of York and his allies against whom Andrew Trollope and his troops turned swiftly and so did the people sent by him the night before to the town [castle]. Died there the Duke of York and the Earl of Rutland his son, the Earl of Salisbury and Sir Thomas his son as well as a couple of lords accompanying them. This battle took place in front of the town of Wakefield on December 31st, 1460. Queen Margaret was very satisfied with the outcome of the battle as well as all the people supporting her cause.

On the other hand the Earls of March and Warwick who had lost their fathers were very moved and concerned . . . '

Recuil des Chroniques D'Engleterre (1891), pp. 324–6.

JOHN S. DAVIES

The work credited to Davies actually refers to the nineteenth-century editor of this fifteenth-century work.

His edited account is as follows:

. . . and anon after the said Duke of York, the Earl of Rutland his son, and the Earl of Salisbury, a little before Christmas, with a few persons went in to the north also, for to repress the malaice of the northern men the which loved not the said Duke of York ne the Earl of Salisbury, and were lodged at the castle of Sandal and at Wakefield.

Then the Lord Neville, brother to the Earl of Westmorland, under false colour went to the said Duke of York, desiring a commission of him for to raise a people for to chastise the rebels of the county; and the duke it granted, deeming that he had true and on his part. When he had his commission he raised a number of 8,000 men, and brought them to the lords of the country; that is to say, The Earl of Northumberland, Lord Clifford, and Duke of Somerset, that were adversaries and enemies to Duke Richard. And when they saw a convenient time for to fill yheir crul intent, the last day of December they fell upon the said Duke Richard, and him killed, and his son th'Earl of Rutland, and many other knights and squires; that is to say, the Lord Harrington a young man, Thomas Harrington Knight, Sir Thomas Neville son of th'Earl of Salisbury, and Sir Harry Radford knight; and of other people to the number of 2,200.

The Earl of Salisbury was taken alive, and led by the said Duke of Somerset to the castle of Pomfret, and for a great sum of money that he should have paid for grant of his life. But the common people of the county which loved him not, took him from the castle by violence and smote off his head.

An English Chronicle of the reigns of Richard II, Henry IV, V, VI (Camden Society, 1856), pp. 106–7.

POLYDORE VERGIL

Polydore Vergil was an Italian who came to England and composed a history at the invitation of Henry VIII. He received information from contemporaries of the event, and he gives an account of the battle of Wakefield, with a list of the slain. His work was first published in 1534.

His account is as follows:

> After these things the Duke of York, knowing for certaine that the queen would
> not be content with the decree of this parliament [appointing him successor to
> the crown] made speede into Yorkshire to pursue her, and pitched his campe at
> a towne distant from York upon the west about fifteen miles, of some strength,
> by reason of a castle adjoying, which towne is called Wakefield; and there he
> consulted with his friends as touching the assaling of his enemyes. Some there
> were who thought it not well to joyne battaile before his sonne Edward should
> come with newe forces; but the duke, trusting to his owne knowledge in
> warfare, and the valience of his soldiers, yssued out of his campe against his
> enemyes in good array.
>
> Likewise the queen, who was resolved in minde to demand her husbande by
> dint of swoorde, and for that cause had alreadie assembled a puissant armie,
> against them and gave them the charge. At the beginning the fight was mightily
> mainteyned mutually, while that a great part of them who were in the front
> battaile being killed, the Duke of Yorkes small number was environed of the
> multitude. Then the queen, encouraging her men, vanquished the residue of
> her enemyes in the moment of one houre. There fell in that conflict Richarde,
> Duke of Yorke, the head of that faction, with Edmund his sonne, Earle of
> Rutlande, Thomas Neville, David Hall, John Parre, Walter Limbrike, John
> Gedding, Eustace Wentworth, Guy Harrington, of thorder of Knights, and of
> courageous Captains James Fitzjames, Ralphe Hastings, John Baunne, and
> Roland Digbie.
>
> Richard, erle of Salisbury, another head of that faction, was amoungst other
> taken, who were beheaded soone after, and their heades, put upon stakes were
> carried to Yorke for a spectacle to the people, and a terror to the rest of their
> adversaryes.'

Three Books of Polydore Vergil's English History, ed. Sir H. Ellis (Camden Society,
1844), pp. 108–9.

EDWARD HALL

> Edward Hall derives some authority from his having been a descendent of Sir
> David Hall, the friend and councillor of the Duke of York. But his chronicle is
> gossiping and unreliable, and he puts long imaginary speeches into the mouths
> of his characters. Hall's Chronicle was published by Grafton in 1548 . . . Hall
> has been used by nearly all modern historians, and the version of the battle told
> by him is now the one generally received.

His account is as follows:

> The Duke of York well knowing, that the queen would spurn and impugne the
> conclusions agreed and taken in this parliament, caused her and her son, to be
> sent for by the king: but she being a manly woman, wishing to rule and not be

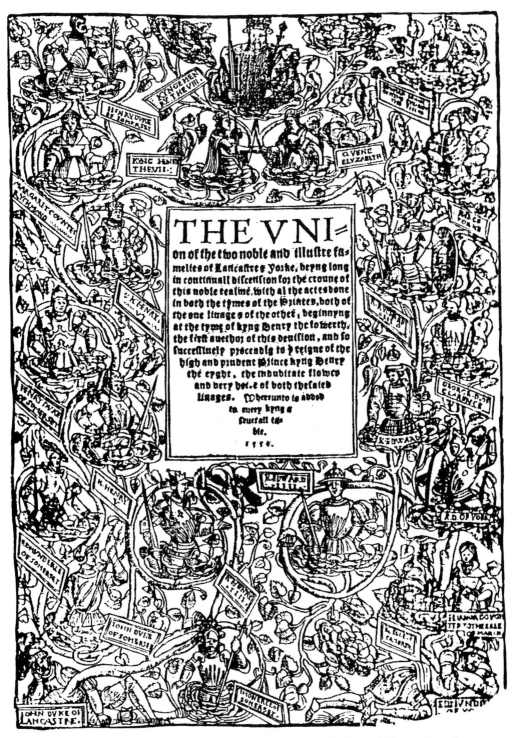

Frontispiece to Edward Hall's chronicle, The Union of the Two Noble and Illustre Famelies etc *(London, 1550). It shows the family trees of the two opposing Yorkist and Lancastrian families united by the figure of Henry VIII (top). (G. Wheeler)*

ruled, & there to counselled by the Dukes of Exeter and Somerset, not only denied to come, but also assembled together a great army, intending to take the king by fine force, out of the lords hands, and set them to a new school. The protector lying in London, having perfect knowledge of all these doings; assigned the Duke of Norfolk and the Earl of Warwick, his trusted friends, to be about the king, and he with the Earls of Salisbury, and Rutland: with a convenient company, departed out of London, the second date of December northward, and sent to the Earl of March his eldest son to follow him with all his power.

The duke by small journeys, came to his castle of Sandal, besides Wakefield, on Christmas Eve, and there began to assemble his tenants and friends. The queen being thereof ascertained, determined to couple with him while his power was small and his aid not come: And so, having in her company, the prince her son, the Dukes of Exeter and Somerset, the Earl of Devonshire, the Lord Clifford, the Lord Roos, and in effect all the Lords of the North part, with eighteen thousand men, or as some [would] write, twenty and two thousand, marched from York to Wakefield, and bade base to the duke, even before his castle; he, having with him not five thousand persons, determined incontinent to issue out, and to fight with his enemies, and although, Sir Davy Hall, his old servant and chief counseillor, advised him to keep his castle and to defend the same with his small number till his son the Earl of March were come with his power of Marchmen and Welsh soldiers; yet he would not be counselled, but in a great fury said, 'Ah Davy, Davy, hast thou loved me so long, and now would'st have me dishonoured? Thou never saw me keep fortress when I was Regent of Normandy, when the Dauphin himself, with his puissance came to besiege me, but like a man, and not like a bird included in a cage, I issued and fought with my enemies, to their loss ever (I thank God) and to my honour. If I have not kept my self within walls for fear of a great and strong prince, nor hid my face from any man living, wouldst thou that I, for dread of a scolding woman, whose weapon is only her tongue, and her nails, should incarcerate myself, and shut my gates? Then all men might of me wonder and all creatures may of me report dishonour, that a woman hath made me dastard, whom no man ever to this day could yet prove a coward: And surely my mind is rather to die with honour, than to live with shame; for of honour cometh fame, and of dishonour riseth infamy. Their great number shall not appal my spirits, but encourage them; for surely I think that I have there as many friends as enemies, which at joining, will either fly or take my part. Therefore advance my banner, in the name of God and St George, for surely I will fight with them, though I should fight alone.'

The Earl of Salisbury and other of his friends, seeing his courage, resolved themselves to his opinion, and ordered their men, and set them forth in warlike fashion, for their most advantage. The Duke of Somerset and other of the queen's part knowing perfectly that if the duke got the victory, their days were finished, and their livings left bare, like men quickened and exasperate, for the safeguard of their lives and defence of their goods, determined to abide the chance, and to espespy their most advantage, and so appointed the Lord

Clifford, to lie in the one stole [ambush], and the Earl of Wiltshire in the other, and they themselves kept the main battle.

The Duke of York with his people, descended down the hill in good order and array and was suffered to pass forward, toward the main battle: but when he was in the plain ground between his castle and the town of Wakefield, he was environed [surrounded] on every side, like a fish in a net, or a deer in a buck-stall; so that he, manfully fighting, was within half an hour slain and dead, and his whole army discomfited, and with him died of his trusty friends, his two bastard uncles, Sir John & Sir Hugh Mortimer, Sir Davy Hall his chief counsellor, Sir Hugh Hastings, Sir Thomas Neville, William and Thomas Parre, both brethren, and two thousand and eight hundred other, whereof many were young gentlemen, and heirs of great parentage in the south part, whose lineages revenged their deaths, within four months next [at Towton] immediately ensuing . . .

. . . In this conflict was wounded and taken prisoner, Richard Earl of Salisbury, Sir Richard Lymbrike, Ralph Stanley, John Harrow, Captain Hauson, and many other. While this battle was in fighting, a priest called Sir Robert Aspall, chaplain and schoolmaster to the young Earl of Rutland second son to the above named Duke of York, scarce of the age of twelve years, a fair gentleman and a maidenlike person, perceiving that flight was more safeguard than tarrying, both for him and his master, secretly conveyed the earl out of the field, by the Lord Clifford's band towards the town, but ere he could enter into a house, he was by the said Lord Clifford spied, followed, and taken, and by reason of his appearance, demanded what he was.

The young gentleman, dismayed, had not a word to speak, but kneeled on his knees imploring mercy, and desiring grace, both with holding up his hands and making dolorous countenance, for his speech was gone for fear. 'Save him,' said his chaplain, 'for he is a prince's son, and eradventure may do you good hereafter.' With that word, the Lord Clifford marked him and said: 'By God's blood, thy father slew mine, and so I will do thee and all thy kin,' and with that word, struck the earl to the heart with his dagger, and bade his chaplain bear the earl's mother and brother word of what he had done, and said. In this act the Lord Clifford was labelled a tyrant, and no gentleman; for the property of the lion, which is furious and unreasonable beast, is to be cruel to them that withstand him, and gentle to such as prostrate or humiliate themselves before him.

Yet this cruel Clifford and deadly Bloodsupper not content with this homicide, or child-killing came to the place where the dead corpse of the Duke of York lay, and caused his head to be stricken off, and set upon it a crown of paper, and so fixed it on a pole, and presented it to the queen, not lying far from the field, in great despite, and much derision, saying: 'Madam, your war is done, here is your king's ransom,' at which present, was much joy, and great rejoicing, but many laughed then that sore lamented after – as the queen herself, and her son. And many were glad then of other men's deaths, not knowing that their own was near at hand – as the Lord Clifford, and other. But surely, man's nature is so frail, that things passed be some forgotten, and mischief's to come, be not foreseen.

After this victory by the queen and her part obtained, she caused the Earl of Salisbury, with all the other prisoners, to be sent to Pontefract and there to be beheaded, and sent all their heads, and the Duke's head of York, to be set upon poles, over the gate of the city of York, in despite of them and their lineage, whose children shortly revenged their father's quarrel, both to the queen's extreme perdition, and the utter undoing of her husband and son.

This end had the valiant lord, Richard Plantagenet, Duke of York.

Hall's Chronicle, ed. H. Ellis (1809), pp. 249–51.

JOHN STOW

John Stow, who was born in 1525, wrote his chronicle between 1560 and 1600; he is an authority by great weight of reason of the diligence and care with which he conducted his researches. He gives one or two particulars, connected with the battle, that are not found elsewhere.

His account is as follows:

The Duke of York protector being at London, assigned the Duke of Norfolk, and the Earl of Warwick his trusted friends, to be about the king, and he with the Earl of Salisbury and the Earl of Rutland, and a convenient number of men, departed out of London, the second of December, and sent to the Earl of March his eldest son to follow him with all his power. The duke came to the castle of Sandal besides Wakefield on Christmas Eve, and there began to assemble his tenants and friends. There came to him under the colour of friendship, the Lord Neville, brother of the Earl of Westmorland, and requested of him a commission for him to raise the people for to chastise his rebels, as he laid; but when he had rallied to the number of 8,000 men, he brought them to the Lords of the county, that is to say, the Earl of Northumberland and the rest.

The queen ascertained thereof, determined to meet him before his power were come together, and to, having in her company the prince her son, the Duke of Exeter and Somerset, the Earl of Devonshire, the lord Clifford, the Lord Roos, and in effect all the Lords of the North party with 18,000 men, marched from York to Wakefield where they placed themselves even before the castle gates. The duke having with him some fully 5,000 Men contrary to the mind of his faithful friends would needs issue forth to fight with his enemies. The Duke of Somerset and others of the queen's part, deuifed, how to take them, and to appointed the Lord Clifford to lie on the one side, and the Earl of Wiltshire in the other, and the duke with other kept the main battle.

The Duke of York with his people descended down the hill in good order of array, and had suffered to pass on toward the main battle: but when he was in the plain field between his castle and the town of Wakefield, he was environed on every side, so that he manfully fighting was within half hour slain, and his whole army discomforted: and with him died of his true friends, his two bastard uncles Sir John, and Sir Hugh Mortimer, Sir David Hall, Sir Hugh Hastings and Sir Thomas Neville son to the Earl of Salisbury, William and Thomas a Parre, brethren, Lord Harrington knight, Sir Henry Ratford knight, and others to the number of 2,200. Whereof many were young gentlemen, and being of great parentage in the south parts. In this conflict was wounded and taken prisoner Richard Earl of Salisbury and was led by the Duke of Somerset to the castle of Pontefract, and had grant of life for a great ransom, but the common people of the country, who loved him not, took him out of the castle by violence and smote off his head. There was also taken Sir Richard Limbrike, Ralph Stanley, John Harrow, Captain Hanson.

The Lord Clifford perceiving where the Earl of Rutland was conveyed out of the field, by one of his father chaplains, and followed and overtook him, and stabbed him to death with a dagger as he kneeled before him. The same Lord Clifford not satisfied herewith, came to the place where the dead corps of the Duke of York lay, and caused his head to be stricken off, and set on it a crown of paper and fixed it on a pole, and presented it to the queen, not lying far from the field. The duke's head with the Earl of Salisbury were set upon a gate of York. This battle was fought southward of Wakefield, by the fair stone bridge of nine arches, on the last day of December. Those of Wakefield shall be shown in my career volume that is to come God willing.

Annales, or a Generall Chronicle of England (1615), pp. 683–5.

Combatants, Casualties and Commanders

In common with all other battles from this period, Wakefield is open to debate on such questions as who was present, how many combatants were involved, and who was killed during the engagement. In terms of the numbers present on the field of battle, Hall gives figures of 5,000 Yorkists, and 18,000 Lancastrians, although he does add in his chronicle the phrase, 'or as some would write twenty and two thousand', although he does not specify precisely who claimed the higher figure.

Benet in his chronicle puts the Lancastrians at 20,000 and the Yorkists at 12,000. William Gregory gives no figure for the Yorkists but numbers the Lancastrians at 15,000. Alternatively William of Worcester gives no figure for the Lancastrians but puts the Yorkists at 6,000. The author of *An English Chronicle of the reigns of Richard II, Henry IV, V, VI* claims that John Neville brought 8,000 men to the battle, apparently on the Yorkist side (although he sided with the Lancastrians on the field). However, it is difficult to quantify this figure and it is not known for certain whether this number is included by the chroniclers in the Lancastrian figures mentioned above. If not, then the increased figure for the Lancastrians could be as many as 30,000, based on the 22,000 mentioned by Hall.

In summary, taking a realistic look at the statements made above, the number of combatants present on the field of battle should be taken as follows: there were between 5,000 and 6,000 Yorkists, and between 15,000 and 22,000 Lancastrians, bringing the total numbers engaged on the day to somewhere between 20,000 and 28,000 but certainly not more than 30,000.

As to the casualties, it was usual for the losing side to suffer the most, and generally these losses occurred during the rout. There is no mention as such of casualties amongst the Lancastrians although it is certain that they sustained some. As for the Yorkists, according to Hall they suffered 2,800 killed, although William of Worcester puts the figure rather more conservatively at 2,000; William Gregory and John Stow both settle for a figure between 2,200 and 2,500.

As such, and including an estimate for the Lancastrians, we should number the casualties as follows: there were between 2,000 and 2,500 Yorkists, and somewhere between 200 and 500 Lancastrians. Therefore, the total casualties on the day were

Detail of the memorial brass to Thomas Colt (d. 1471) in Royden, Essex, showing the indent which once held an enamelled Yorkist livery collar. He was wounded at Wakefield by his rival, Roger Thorpe. (C.E.J. Smith)

probably between 2,500 and 2,800 but certainly no more than 3,000. This figure in effect represents 1 in 10 of those present that day.

As to who was actually present on the field of battle, we are fortunate to have a mass of information, mainly from the chroniclers, the Paston Letters and the Act of Attainder issued by Edward IV after the battle of Towton (*see* Appendix IV).

With reference to the commanders killed, the chroniclers claim the following 'died for the cause of the white rose':

Polydore Vergil	**Edward Hall**
Killed:	Killed:
Duke of York	Duke of York
Earl of Rutland	Earl of Rutland
Sir Thomas Neville	Sir Thomas Neville
Sir David Hall	Sir David Hall

The effigy of Queen Margaret's faithful companion, who as 'Robert Whityngham, Knyght' is named in the Act of Attainder as having fought at Wakefield. His tomb is at Aldbury Church, Herts., where he was buried after his death at Tewkesbury in 1471.

Sir John Parre
Sir John Gedding
Sir Eustace Wentworth
Sir Guy Harrington
Sir Ralph Hastings
Captain Fitz-James
Captain John Baunne
Captain Roland Digby
Walter Lymbrike

Captured:

Earl of Salisbury

William of Worcester

Killed:

Duke of York
Sir Thomas Neville
Sir Thomas Parre
Sir Edward Bourchier
Sir James Pickering
Sir Thomas Harrington
Captain Rathford

Captured:

Earl of Salisbury
Sir Ralph Stanley
Captain Hanson[2]
Walter Lymbrike

Sir William Parre
Sir Thomas Parre
Sir Hugh Hastings
Sir John Mortimer
Sir Hugh Mortimer

Captured:

Earl of Salisbury
Sir Ralph Stanley
Captain Hauson (Hanson?)
Walter Lymbrike
John Harrow

John Stow

Killed:

Duke of York
Sir Thomas Neville
Sir David Hall
Sir William Parre[1]
Sir Thomas Parre
Sir John Mortimer
Sir Hugh Mortimer
Sir Henry Ratford
Sir Thomas Harrington
Lord Harrington
Sir Hugh Hastings

Captured:

Sir Ralph Stanley
Captain Hanson
Walter Lymbrike
John Harrow[3]

The chroniclers do not mention any Yorkists who were captured and not subsequently put to death. However, Barrett wrote the following interesting note:

> According to a well-substantiated tradition, the Wakefield Tower, in the Tower of London, owes its name to having been used as a prison for some of the

Drawing from Dugdale's Warwickshire *of memorial window figures to Sir William Feilding and his wife Agnes. Feilding probably fought at Wakefield, as he was specifically excluded from Edward IV's pardon proclamation afterwards. He fell fighting for the Lancastrians at Tewkesbury in 1471. (G. Wheeler)*

captives taken in the fight. The prison room is never shown to the public, being as it is beneath the present Jewel House. The Wakefield Tower adjoins (on the east side) the so-called Bloody Tower. Its basement room is entered through a small, low, and narrow-arched door, concealed by one of the huge gates of the Bloody Tower, which when open are locked back to the wall on either side.

On obtaining admittance, the front room, which is beneath the Bloody Tower, is seen to be furnished with one or two cupboard recesses in its walls. This was in former times the dwelling of the executioner. A smaller room off it contains the remains of the circular stone stair, leading to the upper part of Bloody Tower. By the door, entrance is gained to the basement prison room – a room with a vaulted roof supported by a central pillar.

The Wakefield Tower is circular on the outside but polygonal within, some sides being pierced by deep embrasures and lighted by tiny windows. Into this hole the wretched captives were probably thrust. The present jewel room above has in its wall an interesting little oratory, with a piscina on the south side of the space where the altar once stood. This room is traditionally the scene of the murder of Henry VI.[4]

This alabaster effigy in St Peter's Church, Martley, Worcs., is said to be of Sir Hugh Mortimer who, according to Edward Hall's chronicle, was slain at Wakefield. Research has shown that he actually died some months before the battle. (B. Benstead)

Although this makes interesting reading, it is unlikely to be true because London itself and the Tower were held by the Yorkists from a point before the battle of Wakefield until well afterwards.

There is no mention of any casualties amongst the Lancastrian commanders, but the following chroniclers give the nobles listed below as being present on the field of battle:

Edward Hall:
Duke of Somerset, Earl of Northumberland, Lord Clifford, Earl of Devon, Lord Roos, Duke of Exeter, Earl of Wiltshire.

William of Worcester:
Duke of Somerset, Earl of Northumberland, Lord Clifford, Lord Neville, Andrew Trollope, Duke of Exeter.

John S Davies, editor of *An English Chronicle of the reigns of Richard II, Henry IV, V, VI*:
Duke of Somerset, Lord Neville, Earl of Northumberland, Lord Clifford.

This effigy at Methley Church, Yorkshire, is of Lionel, Lord Welles. He was probably present at Wakefield, according to Markham, and he was killed at Towton in 1461. (G. Wheeler)

William Gregory:
Duke of Somerset, Lord Neville, Lord Clifford, Lord Latimer, Earl of Devon, Alexander Hody, Lord Roos, 'Baron' Greystock, Duke of Exeter.

In the various papers written on the battle of Wakefield, a number give a good account of who was present, but they do not, in all instances, inform us of where they got their information. For example, the historian Markham mentions present on the field for the Lancastrians:

Thomas Fulford, James Luttrel, John de Vere, Earl of Oxford, James Butler, Earl of Wiltshire,[5] Sir Richard Tempest, Lord Dacre of Gillesland, plus members from the following families: Fortescue, Hungerford, Welles, Beaumont and Plumpton.[6]

Also, Barrett mentions that Sir James Strangeways was present for the Yorkists, whereas for the Lancastrians, that the following knighted the said people on the field of battle after their victory:

The Duke of Somerset knighted: Lord Clifford, James Lutterell, Robert Whittingham, Nicholas Latymer.

Garter stall plate to Sir Richard Tunstall KG, St George's Chapel, Windsor. Tunstall fought at Wakefield and Towton, after which he escaped with Queen Margaret, and was attainted in 1461. After surrendering Harlech Castle to the Yorkists in 1468, he changed sides, adhering to Edward IV and Richard III. He died in 1492. (G. Wheeler)

The Earl of Northumberland knighted: Richard Percy (his brother), William Gascoigne, Thomas Metham, William Bertram, Richard Alborough, Thomas Elderton, John Malev'er, William St Quintyn.

The Earl of Devon knighted: John Courtenay, (his brother) Thomas Fulford, Alexander Hody, Richard Cary.

Clifford then in turn knighted: Rodger Clifford, Richard Tempest, Henry Bellingham.

Lord Roos then knighted: Thomas Babthorpe.[7, 8]

It seems reasonable to assume that those who were knighted on the day of the battle by others reported as present by the chroniclers, must have been participants in the engagement.

APPENDIX IV

The Act of Attainder

The following is a resume of the Act of Attainder which was issued by Edward IV after the battle of Towton, on 29 March 1461. It was in many ways not only a political requirement, especially in light of Edward IV's overwhelming victory at Towton, but was also widely believed to have been an act of revenge against those who had taken part in the battle of Wakefield and brought about the death of his father, the Duke of York. Indeed, one can almost feel the hatred in the comments made in the compilation of the summary of the act, which reads as follows:

For asmoch also as Henry duc of Somerset, purposying, ymaginyng and compassying of extreme and insaciate malice and violence to destroy the right noble and famous Prynce of wur memorie Richard late Duc of York, Fader to oure Liege and Soverayne Lord Kyng Edward the fourth, and in his lyf verey Kyng in right of the realme of Englond, singuler Protectour Lover and Defensour of the good governaunce, pollicie, commyn wele, peas and tranquillite thereof; and also Thomas Courteney late Erle of Devonshire, Henry late Erle of Nortumberland, Thomas Lord Roos, John late Lord Nevill, John Welpdale late of Lychefeld Clerk, Philip Lowes late of Thouresby in the countie of Lincoln Clerk, Bawdewyn Fufforth Knyght, Alexander Hody Knyght, Nicolas Latymer Knyght, Thomas Fyndern Knyght, Henry Lewes Knyght, John Heron of the Forde Knyght, Richard Tunstall Knyght, Henry Belyngeham Knyght, Robert Whityngham Knyght, William Grymmesby late of London late Squier, Thomas Tunstall late of Thurland in the shire of Lancastr' Squier, Symond hamomes Knyght, Thomas Dalton late of Lilbourne in the counte of Northumberlond Gentilman, James Dalton late of same Gentilman, John Clapam late of Skipton in Craven in Yorkshire Yoaman, Andrew Trollop late of Guysnes Squire, Antony Notehill Knyght, John Botiller, late of Howke in the counte of Dorset Squier, Gawen Lampleugh late of York Taylleour, Thomas Frysell late of the same Smyth, John Smothyng late of the same Yoman, John Caterall late of Brayton in the counte of York Gentilman, William Fyppes late of Southduffield in the counte of Yorke Yoman, Henry Clyff the elder late of Lokyngton in the counte of York Yoman, Robert Tomlynson late of Helagh in the counte of York Yoman, and Thomas Barton late of York Mason; at Wakefield in the shire of York on Tywesday

XXX day Decembr' last past (1460), with grete despite and cruell violence, horrible and unmanly tyrannye murdered the seid right noble Prynce Duc of York.

Rot. Par. 1st Edward IV (1461), vol. V, p. 477.

APPENDIX V

The Neville–Lovelace Scenario

One of the myths born from the battle of Wakefield concerns one Captain Lovelace from Kent. It was during the subsequent second battle of St Albans, that the Yorkist army, under the field command of the Earl of Warwick ('The Kingmaker'), came under attack from the Lancastrian army under the command of the Duke of Somerset and Margaret of Anjou (but in essence) directed by Andrew Trollope.

The left flank of the Yorkist army, which was stationed within and around St Albans, and commanded by Sir John Neville, brother to the Earl of Warwick, bore the brunt of the Lancastrian attack, the remainder of the Yorkist army having taken up an extended position east of the town of St Albans beyond Barnard's Heath. During this attack the whole of the Lancastrian army came down upon the men under Sir John Neville's command, who, even though vastly outnumbered, still managed to hold their ground for some considerable time, while messengers were sent to the Earl of Warwick informing him of the attack and the precarious position that John Neville's force now found themselves facing.

While waiting for reinforcements to arrive, a portion of John Neville's men (said to number some 500 men), and allegedly under the command of Lovelace, did, in the heat of battle, declare for the house of Lancaster and changed sides. Although this was a practice not uncommon during the Wars of the Roses, in this instance it had a devastating effect on the hard-pressed men under John Neville's command. Their morale broke and they scattered, and the subsequent rout resulted in the Yorkist defeat, the capture of Sir John Neville and the 'liberation' of King Henry VI, who had 'enjoyed' the 'protection' of his Yorkist cousins since his capture at the battle of Northampton the previous year.

It is claimed that the reason for Lovelace's change of sides stemmed from the battle of Wakefield, where he fought for the house of York but was captured by the Lancastrians. It is also claimed that in return for his life and before he was set free and brought the news to Warwick in London of the defeat at Wakefield and the deaths of the Duke of York and the Earl of Salisbury, he had to swear an oath of allegiance to Henry VI and promise to betray the Yorkists at 'an opportune moment'. That moment seems to have come during the second battle of St Albans.

However, the whole story becomes suspect because the name Lovelace does not appear in any correspondence or chronicle regarding actions or incidents before or after the battle of Wakefield. There is a tenuous reference to Lovelace's role at the second battle of St Albans in *The English Chronicle*, pp. 107–8, but he is not included in the Act of Attainder issued by Edward IV after the battle of Towton.

The only chronicler who mentions him at all is de Waurin, who wrote about the battle of St Albans:

> . . . As the Queen Margaret who was subtil and malicious did so much in donations and promises to a man named Lovelace Captain of Kent, that he turned against the Earl of Warwick. The captain Lovelace was the man he trusted the most . . .[1]

It is not to be doubted that it was men like Lord Wenlock, Sir Robert Ogle and Sir William and Sir John Conyers, who were the earl's most trusted captains. Indeed, their names are frequently mentioned in the text of the chroniclers and historians from all ages as being so. This obviously sheds some doubt on de Waurin's opinion that Lovelace was the man Warwick 'trusted the most'. Therefore, it is suggested that this entire Lovelace 'scenario' was created by the Earl of Warwick to mask what is generally agreed to have been his total mismanagement of the St Albans campaign. He had until then remained undefeated in battle, and the rout at St Albans was a severe blow to Yorkist morale. This being the case, the Earl of Warwick – using the whole might of the Yorkist propaganda machine – 'created' Lovelace to take the blame for his defeat and so the Neville–Lovelace scenario was born.

There is little or no evidence either way - I leave it to the reader to make up his or her own mind.

APPENDIX VI

Sources

Contemporary and near-contemporary sources:

Fabyan, R. *The New Chronicles of England and France* ed. H.T. Ellis (1811).

Gregory, William. 'Gregory's Chronicle' in *The Historical Collections of a Citizen of London*, ed. J. Gairdner (Camden Society, 1876), pp. 2108-10.

Hall, Edward. *Hall's Chronicle*, ed. H. Ellis (1809), pp. 249-51.

Leland, John. *Itinerary* (1558); (The Yorkshire extracts, as shown in Yorkshire Archaeological Journal 1889), vol. 10, pp. 241–2).

Stow, John. *Annales, or a Generall Chronicle of England* (1615), pp. 683– 4.

Vergil, Polydore. *Three Books of Polydore Vergil's English History*, ed. Sir H. Ellis (Camden Society, 1844).

William of Worcester. *Annales Rerum Angelicarum*, vol. II pp. 484–5. (Translation as shown in *The Chronicles of the White Rose of York*, vol. LXXXIII, ed. J.C. Giles, 1843.

Jean de Waurin. *Recuil des Chroniques D' Engleterre*, eds W. Hardy and E. Hardy (1891).

Whethamstede, J. *Registrum Abbatis*, ed. H.T. Riley (1872).

Principal sources:

Croyland Abbey Chronicle, ed. Nicholas Proney and John Cox (Richard III & Yorkist History Trust, 1986).

Three fifteenth-century Chronicles, ed. J. Gairdner (Camden Society, 1880).

Rotuli Parliamentorum, 6 vols (Record Commission, 1767).

Calendar of Charter Rolls, vol. VI (1427–1516), 1927.

Calendar of State Papers and Manuscripts existing in the archives and collections of Milan, vol. I (1385–1618), ed. A.B. Hinds.

Calendar of Close Rolls, Henry VI (1454–1461), 1967.

Calendar of Patent Rolls, Henry VI (1454–1461), 1911.

The Great Chronicle of London, ed. A.H. Thomas and I.D. Thornly, 1938.

An English Chronicle of the reigns of Richard II, Henry IV, V, VI, ed. John S. Davies (Camden Society, 1856), pp. 107–8.

York Civic Records, ed. A. Raines (Yorkshire Archaeological Society, Record Series, vol. 98, 1939).

The Chronicles of the Wars of the Roses, ed. Elizabeth Hallam (Weidenfeld and Nicholson, 1992).

Barrett, C.R.B. *Battles and Battlefields in England* (Innes, 1896), pp. 131–40.

Boardman, A. *The Battle of Towton* (Sutton Publishing, 1993), pp. 26–32.

Brooke, R. *Visits to the Fields of Battles in England* (John Russell Smith, 1857), pp. 53–65.

Freeman, E.A. *The Battles of Wakefield* (1894), pp. 275–83.

Goodman, A. *The Wars of the Roses* (Routledge, 1981), pp. 41–4.

Johnson, P.A. *Richard Duke of York, 1411–60* (Oxford University Press, 1988), pp. 218–24.

Leadman, A.D.H. 'The Battle of Wakefield', *Yorkshire Archaeological Journal*, vol. XI, 1891, pp. 348–60.

Markham, C.R. 'The Battle of Wakefield', *Yorkshire Archaeological Journal*, vol. IX, 1886, pp. 105–23.

Stanfield, A. 'Sandal Castle and the Battle of Wakefield' (A paper read before the Wakefield Photographic Society,1891.

Tyas, G. *The Battles of Wakefield*, 1854, pp. 48–61.

Secondary sources:

Butler, L. *Sandal Castle – Wakefield* (Wakefield Historical Society, 1991), pp. 50–1.

Burne, A.H. *Battlefields of England* (Methuen, 1950).

Burne, A.H. *More Battlefields of England* (Methuen, 1952).

Carpenter, C. *Locality and Polity* (Cambridge, 1992).

Chrimes, S.B. *Lancastrians, Yorkists, and Henry VII* (London, 1964).

Crowther, G.H. *A Descriptive History of the Wakefield Battles* (1886), pp. 16–22.

Dockray, K. and Knowles, R. *The Battle of Wakefield* (Richard III Society, 1993).

Gairdner, J. *The Paston Letters* (Sutton Publishing, 1986).

Gillingham, J. *The Wars of the Roses* (Weidenfeld Paperbacks, 1990), pp. 118–22.

Gransden, A. *Historical Writings in England* (London, 1982).

Griffith, P. *The Battle of Blore Heath* (Paddy Griffith Associates, 1995).

Griffiths, R.A. 'Local Rivalries and National Politics: The Percies and the Nevilles, and the Duke of Exeter, 1452–1455', *Speculum* no. 43, 1968.

Giles, J.C. *The Chronicles of the White Rose of York* (1843).

Haigh, P.A. *Military Campaigns of the War of the Roses* (Sutton Publishing, 1995), pp. 31–9.

Hammond, P.W. *The Battles of Barnet and Tewkesbury* (Sutton Publishing, 1990).

Hammond/Sutton/Visser-Fuchs. 'The Reburial of Richard Duke of York 21–30 July 1476', *The Ricardian*, vol. X, no. 127, 1994.

Hicks, M. *Bastard Feudalism* (Longman Press, 1995).

Hibbert, C. *Agincourt* (Windrush, 1995).

Hodges, G. *Ludford Bridge and Mortimer's Cross* (Longaston Press, 1989).

Jones, Dr 'York, Somerset and the Wars of the Roses', *English History Review*, 1989.

Jack, RI. 'The Battle of Northampton, July 10th 1460', *Northamptonshire Past and Present*, vol. III, no I, 1960.

Kendall, P.M. *Warwick the Kingmaker and the Wars of the Roses* (Sphere Books, 1972).

Kinross, J. *Walking and Exploring the Battlefields of England* (Davis and Charles, 1993).

Kingsford, C.L. *English Historical Literature in the 15th Century* (Oxford, 1913).

Lander, J.R. *The Wars of the Roses* (Sutton Publishing, 1993).

Lander, J.R. *Henry VI and the Duke of York's Second Protectorate* (B.J.R.L. vol. XLIII, 1960).

McFarlane, K.B. *England in the Fifteenth Century* (Hambledon, 1981).

Oman, C., Sir. *The Art of War in the Middle Ages* (Greenhill Books, vol. 2, 1991).

Pollard, R.A.J. 'Percies and Nevilles', *History Today*, Sept. 1993.

Powick, M.R. *Military Obligations in Medieval England* (Oxford University Press, 1962).

Ray, P. 'English Civil War', *Notes and Queries*, vol. 44, pp. 3–7.

Ramsay, J., Sir. *Lancaster and York* (Oxford, vol. II, 1892), pp. 236–9.

Ross, C. *Edward IV* (Methuen, 1991).

Ross, C. 'The Estates and Finances of Richard Duke of York', *Welsh History Review*, vol. III, 1967.

Ross, C. *The Wars of the Roses* (Thames and Hudson, 1986).

Smurthwaite, D. *Complete Guide to the Battlefields of Britain* (Mermaid Books, 1993).

Scofield, C.L. *The Life and Reign of Edward IV* (vol. I, 1923).

Speed, J. *The Counties of Britain, A Tudor Atlas by John Speed* (1988).

Story, R.L. *The End of the House of Lancaster* (Barrie and Rockliff, 1966).

Wolffe, B. *Henry VI* (Methuen, 1983).

Walker, J.W. 'St Mary's Chapel on Wakefield Bridge', *Yorkshire Archaeological Journal*, vol. II.

REFERENCES:

Glossary:

Butler	Butler, L. *Sandal Castle – Wakefield*, Wakefield Historical Society, 1991.
Davies	*An English Chronicle of the reigns of Richard II, Henry IV, V, VI*, ed. John S. Davies (Camden Society, 1856).
Gregory	William Gregory, 'Chronicle' in *The Historical Collections of a Citizen of London*, ed. J. Gairdner (C.S., 1876).
Hall	Edward Hall, *Hall's Chronicle*, ed. H. Ellis, 1809.
Leland	John Leland, 'Itinerary', 1558 – The Yorkshire extracts, as shown in *Yorkshire Archaeological Journal*, vol. 10, 1889.
Stow	John Stow, *Annales, or a Generall Chronicle of England*, 1615.
Vergil	Polydore Vergil, *Three Books of Polydore Vergil's English History*, ed. Sir H. Ellis, Camden Society, 1844.
Worc.	William of Worcester, *Annales Rerum Angelicarum*, vol. II, translation as shown in *The Chronicles of the White Rose of York*, LXXXIII, ed. J.C. Giles, 1843.

Barrett   Barrett, C.R.B. *Battles and Battlefields in England* (Innes, 1896).

Brooke   Brooke, R. *Visits to the Fields of Battle in England* (John Russell Smith, 1857).

Freeman   Freeman, E.A. *The Battles of Wakefield*, 1894.

Leadman   Leadman, A.D.H. 'The Battle of Wakefield', *Yorkshire Archaeological Journal*, vol. XI, 1891.

Markham   Markham, C.R. 'The Battle of Wakefield', *Yorkshire Archaeological Journal*, vol. IX, 1886.

Stanfield   Stanfield, A. *Sandal Castle and the Battle of Wakefield*, 1891.

Tyas   Tyas, G. *The Battles of Wakefield*, pp. 48–61, 1854.

Waurin   Jean de Waurin, *Recuil des Chroniques D'Engleterre*, vol. II, eds W. Hardy & E. Hardy, 1891

APPENDIX VII

Further Reading

Below are a few comments regarding a number of other works which mention the battle of Wakefield. They are included here for two reasons. Firstly, to indicate to those who wish to know more about the period in which the battle of Wakefield was fought (the events that led up to the engagement, the battle itself and the consequences thereafter), what they may expect to find in each of the works listed below. Secondly, to illustrate the frustrating lack of military detail to be found in most works about the period. Nevertheless, they remain useful in gaining a wider understanding of the wars.

Barrett, C.R.B. *Battles and Battlefields in England* (1896), pp. 131–40.
    Barrett gives a good account of the battle of Wakefield itself (as well as many other conflicts). He also gives a full list of who was present on the field of battle. Unfortunately he does not complement his text with a map of the battlefield.

Boardman, A. *The Battle of Towton* (1994), pp. 26–32.
    Boardman's work, although primarily on the battle of Towton, is one of the few works that makes more than a passing reference to the battle of Wakefield. His work explores the events that led up to the battles of Wakefield and Towton in detail (including accounts of the battles at St Albans, Blore Heath, Ludford Bridge and Northampton). It is especially useful in terms of explaining why the Duke of York allowed himself to be out-manoeuvred in the Wakefield campaign, and the consequences of the duke's death. Although it does not include a map illustrating the battle of Wakefield, it does contain references to the works of the chroniclers and a number of interesting illustrations regarding key locations on the Wakefield battlefield itself.

Brooke, R. *Visits to the Fields of Battle in England* (1857), pp. 53–65.
    Brooke, who is renowned for his work on the battlefields of Britain, gives a very good account of the battle of Wakefield and complements his text with a liberal sprinkling of quotes from the contemporary chroniclers. He also adds a full list of who was present at the battle. But alas, as in many of his accounts of battles from this period, he does not add a map.

Butler, L. *Sandal Castle – Wakefield* (1991), pp. 50–1.
    Butler gives an excellent account of the history of Wakefield and Sandal Castle.

He also describes in detail the recent archaeological work carried out at the castle. His description of the battle is limited to only half a page but it is concise and to the point. His work, although liberally endowed with photgraphs and diagrams does not contain a map of the battlefield.

Crowther, G.H. *A Descriptive History of the Wakefield Battle* (1886), pp. 16–22.
    The work by Crowther in regards to the battle of 1460, is in fact, a very basic and superficial account, although there is some background information included in his text. His account of the battle itself is not much use to the historian and certainly can not compete with those of Markham and Freeman which were written in the same age.

Freeman, E.A. *The Battles of Wakefield* (1894), pp. 275–83.
    Freeman only includes a limited account of the battle, which is surprising, considering the title of his work. It does contain some accounts by the chroniclers, but no map.

Gillingham, J. *The Wars of the Roses* (1990), pp. 118–22.
    In terms of the military aspects of the Wars of the Roses, Gillingham ranks as one who gives an excellent account in most cases. However, in this instance his account of Wakefield is limited, although he does explore in detail the circumstances surrounding why the duke was drawn into the engagement in the first place. Again there is no map.

Goodman, A. *The Wars of the Roses* (1981).
    For an understanding of the Wars of the Roses, Goodman's work is excellent in exploring the political causes of the wars. His work also covers fifteenth-century military organisation and society. Although the military aspects of the battle of Wakefield are not covered in detail, what makes this work valuable are the references to contemporary and near-contemporary chroniclers and documents which also reinforce his conclusions regarding all aspects of the period.

Haigh, P.A. *Military Campaigns of the Wars of the Roses* (1995).
    It would not be professional to review my own work, but the battle of Wakefield is considered on pp. 31–9. A review can be found in the *Ricardian*.

Johnson, P.A. *Duke Richard of York, 1411–1460* (1988), pp. 218–24.
    Works on the life and times of the Duke of York are difficult to find, but Johnson's work is excellent. It covers all aspects of the duke's life, both social and political as well as his military career. As with Goodman, the military aspects of the battle of Wakefield are only mentioned briefly, but the many references to contemporary and near-contemporary chroniclers and documents make this a valuable book.

Kendall, P.M. *Warwick the Kingmaker and the Wars of the Roses* (1972), pp. 75–6.
    For those who wish to know about the Earl of Warwick and his involvement in

the Wars of the Roses, this is an excellent account. However, the battle of Wakefield is mentioned only briefly.

Kinross, J. *Walking and Exploring the Battlefields of England* (1993), pp. 82–3.

Kinross, in his account of the battle of Wakefield, devotes much of his work on Wakefield to the castle at Sandal, of which he includes a number of photographs and diagrams. Of the battle, he gives very few details, though he gives a good description of the battlefield today and how to walk it. His work contains a map – albeit a basic one.

Lander, J.R. *Wars of the Roses* (1993), pp. 80–3.

Lander's account of the battle is limited, but his work does include the text of the chroniclers and he mentions those who were present. However, as a source for further reading regarding the chronicles (of which the majority of Lander's work consists) it is a valuable work.

Leadman, A.D.H. 'The Battle of Wakefield', *Yorkshire Archaeological Journal*, vol. XI, pp. 348–60.

In my opinion, Leadman's work is the best all-round account of the battle of Wakefield. Not only does this work give a good background, it also includes much of the work of the chroniclers including a full account of who was there and who was killed in the battle. However, his work does not include a map.

Markham, C.R. 'The Battle of Wakefield', *Yorkshire Archaeological Journal*, vol. IX, pp. 105–23, 1886.

Markham, a renowned historian from the last century, supplies a good deal of background information to the Wars of the Roses. He also fully explores the work of the chroniclers, but sadly, gives only a limited account of the engagement. His work does not include a map.

Oman, C., Sir. *The Art of War in the Middle Ages* (vol. II, pp. 412–3); *The Political History of England* (vol. IV 1377–1485, pp. 398–9, 1930).

Although excellent in describing military aspects across a large period of time, unfortunately it mentions the battle of Wakefield in name only. However, the second work dedicates quite a lot of text to the battle and contains some useful information relating to the campaign.

Ramsay, J., Sir. *Lancaster and York* (vol. II, pp. 236–9, 1892).

Ramsay, the great 'modern' chronicler of the Wars of the Roses, sadly gives only a limited account of the battle. His text does include the work of the chroniclers or at least make reference to them, and also mentions who was killed in the conflict. The work does not contain a map.

Ross, C. *Edward IV* (p. 30, 1991).

Charles Ross's work centres mainly around the life of Edward IV, as the title of his book suggests. However, the Wars of the Roses are covered in detail, and as such it is a valuable work to read for those who wish to know more regarding the battles. However, the battle of Wakefield is mentioned only briefly in his work and contains only a few details.

Smurthwaite, D. *Complete Guide to the Battlefields of Britain* (pp. 103–4, 1993).

Although Smurthwaite's work contains the Ordnance Survey map of Sandal and the battlefield, with the troop locations superimposed on it, it is not a detailed account. However, he does describe the battlefield today.

Stanfield, A. *Sandal Castle and the Battle of Wakefield* (1891).

Stansfield's account is written in a very romantic manner and cannot be taken too seriously. He puts words into the mouths of those who were there, but does not give his sources for these statements. His work contains very few details of what actually happened. Although the book contains photographs of the castle at Sandal, it does not contain a map.

Tyas, G. *The Battles of Wakefield* (1854), pp. 48–61.

Tyas's account contains much background information about Wakefield town and the castle, but few details about the actual battle. Again the book contains no map.

Dockray, K. and Knowles, R. *The Battle of Wakefield* (1993).

This recent account of the battle is derived directly from the chroniclers, and other than the fact that the authors do not go beyond what can be proved conclusively, their work is quite informative. There are many useful maps, but because of the previously mentioned reluctance to speculate, or use Burne's IMP theory, no troop movements are indicated. However, their work on the topography of the battlefield is extremely useful in answering some of the hitherto unexplained aspects of the battle.

Notes

Chapter One

1. *London Chronicle for 1446–52*, pp. 297–8.
2. For further reading on Somerset's military ability and his relationship with Richard, Duke of York, I suggest that the reader refers to *York, Somerset and the Wars of the Roses* by Dr Jones (E.H.R., 1989). In this work Jones gives a counter-view to the more common opinion that Somerset was a poor commander. However, despite this, it cannot – in my opinion – be disputed that it was Somerset who was personally responsible for the surrender of the strategic town of Rouen, which subsequently led to the fall of Normandy. For further reading regarding the life of the Duke of York, see P.A. Johnson's *Duke Richard of York, 1411–1460* (Oxford University Press, 1988).
3. For additional information regarding the events of the early 1450s and the beginning of the Wars of the Roses, see R.L Storey's *The End of the House of Lancaster* (Barrie and Rockliff, 1966).
4. There is a multitude of additional reading regarding the Hundred Years War; however, for those who wish to learn more about this period and to gain a broad understanding of the events that took place during this conflict, I suggest that the following books are consulted: C. Allmand (ed.), *The Hundred Years War* (Cambridge University Press, 1988); R. Neillands, *The Hundred Years War* (Routledge, 1990); and K. Fowler, *The Hundred Years War* (Macmillan, 1971). Equally good, from a military point of view, are two works by Burne, *The Crecy War* and *The Agincourt War* (Eyre and Spottiswoode, 1956 and 1958 respectively). For a more recent view of the campaign and battle of Agincourt, I suggest Christopher Hibbert's, *Agincourt* (Windrush, 1995).
5. The long-running feud between the Percys and the Nevilles is covered in A.J. Pollard's article 'The Percys and the Nevilles', published in *History Today*, September 1993, and in R.A. Griffiths' 'Local Rivalries and National Politics: The Percys and the Nevilles, and the Duke of Exeter, 1452–1455', published in *Speculum* no. 43, 1968.
6. Clearly, even today there seems to be a misunderstanding regarding the use of the names Yorkist and Lancastrian in the context of the Wars of the Roses. The names do not reflect a geographical conflict between the County of Yorkshire and the County of Lancaster. The term Wars of the Roses refers to a dynastic struggle between the House of Lancaster (the supporters of Henry VI and his heirs) and the House of York (the supporters of Richard, Duke of York and his heirs). The introduction of roses as symbols for each side was almost certainly a dramatic device introduced by Shakespeare in *Henry VI*, and later immortalized in the painting by Henry Payne, that each side chose a rose as their emblem – a white rose for York and a red rose for Lancaster. It was only long after the event that the conflict became known as the 'Wars of the Roses', apparently christened as such by Sir Walter Scott (*see* the introduction to Lander's *The Wars of the Roses*). If the conflict is to be given any sort of geographical boundaries, then it could loosely be described as a north/south conflict. This is due to the fact that the supporters of the House of Lancaster held lands predominantly in the north (including the majority of the counties of Lancashire, Yorkshire and Northumberland) while the supporters of the House of York held lands along the south coast, etc., in Kent, East Anglia

and the Midlands. On pages 15, 20 and 229 of *The Chronicles of the Wars of the Roses* edited by Elizabeth Hallam (Weidenfield and Nicolson, 1988), there are excellent and simple-to-understand maps which illustrate this point, but equally show how many supporters of both sides held lands within the 'heartlands' of their opponents. This latter point was to be a particular problem for the Duke of York during the Wakefield campaign: while he owned Sandal Castle, the surrounding lands were predominantly held by Lancastrians.

7. *Dijon Relation*, p. 63.
8. For an understanding of the campaign and battle of St Albans 1455, I suggest that the following should be consulted: A.H. Burne's *Battlefields of England* (Methuen, 1950), pp. 75–95, and my own *Military Campaigns of the Wars of the Roses* (Sutton Publishing, 1995), pp. 3–13.
9. For an understanding of the campaign and battle of Blore Heath, I suggest that the following should be consulted: A.H. Burne's *More Battlefields of England* (Methuen, 1952), pp. 140–9, and my own *Military Campaigns of the Wars of the Roses* (Sutton Publishing, 1995), pp. 14–22. The recent publication *The Battle of Blore Heath 1459* edited by Paddy Griffith (Paddy Griffith Associates, 1995), is excellent, as it includes a reprint of an original work, dated 1912, by Colonel F.R. Twemlow.
10. For further reading regarding the campaign and flight from Ludford to Calais, I suggest the work by the late Geoffrey Hodges, *Ludford Bridge and Mortimer's Cross* (Logaston Press, 1989).
11. Davies, pp. 95–7.
12. For an understanding of the campaign and battle of Northampton, I suggest that the following should be consulted: R.I. Jack, *The Battle of Northampton, July 10th 1460* (Northamptonshire Past and Present, III, no I, 1960), and my own *Military Campaigns of the Wars of the Roses* (Sutton Publishing, 1995), pp. 23–30.
13. *Registrum Abbatie*, Whethamstede, pp. 376–8.
14. Waurin, p. 315.
15. A contemporary account of the Duke of York's attempt to gain control of the throne of England can be found in the printed version of the Rolls of Parliament, *Rotuli Parliamentorum*, Royal Commission, 1767, vol. V, (pp. 379–479). The pages mentioned not only cover the events surrounding the Act of Accord, but also the march north to confront the Lancastrians and the attainder issued after the battle of Towton against those who opposed the Yorkists at Wakefield.
16. Goodman, *The Wars of the Roses*, p. 41.

Chapter Two

1. Who were, along with Henry Beaufort, Duke of Somerset, united in their wish for revenge against the Yorkists for the death of their respective fathers at St Albans.
2. Greg, pp. 208–10.
3. Hall, pp. 249–50.
4. Owen Tudor (Owain Ap Maredudd Ap Tudor), had been a squire at the court of Henry V. After Henry's death in 1422, he had become clerk to the wardrobe of Henry's widow, Catherine de Valois. The two married in secret in 1429. By Catherine, Owen had two children, Jasper, later Earl of Pembroke, and Edmund, later Earl of Richmond, and father of Henry VII.
5. See Caroline Barron, *London and the Crown* p. 98. To further confuse the Yorkist leaders, in December they received a letter via the 'Common Council', from the queen, the Prince of Wales and Jasper Tudor, indicating that they may have been in Wales all the while. It is clear from the chronicles that the Yorkists were aware of the Lancastrian activity in the North, but they seem to have been ignorant of the scale of the muster.
6. Vergil, p. 108.
7. His London residence, was Baynard's Castle, where he would stay with the Duchess of York and his children while he was in the capital.
8. Stow, pp. 683–4.
9. Johnson, *Duke Richard Of York 1411–1460*, pp. 218–19.
10. Davies, p. 106.

11. *Registrum Abbatie*, Whethamstede, p. 381.
12. Worc., p. 484.
13. Ibid.
14. The issue of the ravaging and pillaging of York's properties in Yorkshire (as previously mentioned), most notably by Northumberland and Clifford, certainly had a bearing on York's decision to travel north. However, we should not lose sight of the fact that the recovery of northern fortresses – such as Pontefract – was the principal reason for the expedition. Ross, in *Edward IV*, p. 29, wrote: 'by October the [Yorkist] government had been reduced to issuing hopeful commands to a mixed bag of Lancastrian and Yorkist partisans to expel evildoers from these castles [Pontefract in Yorkshire and Penrith in Cumberland], and to call out "lieges of Yorkshire and adjacent counties to storm the same" [CPR 1452–61, 607–8, 610–11] in case of resistance. But there was little hope of success . . .' One could argue that this extract not only supports the view that the Duke of York was heading north to confront the Lancastrians directly at Pontefract, in order to take possession of that fortress, but also that the issue of the plundering of York's estates was a secondary consideration. The previous note regarding artillery also reinforces the view that he was travelling directly to Pontefract, as he would certainly have required artillery to enforce a siege of the castle.
15. Worc., p. 484.
16. Hall, p. 250.
17. Stow, p. 684.
18. Worc., p. 775, *Annales Rerum Anglicarum* vol. II, ed. Stevenson, 1884.
19. The truce is mentioned by the Victorian historian Ramsay, in *Lancaster and York*, p. 237, and by Boardman in *The Battle of Towton*, p. 26, as well as many others.
20. The truce was mentioned by the Abbot of St Albans, who wrote in the *Whethamstede Registar*, p. 381, that the two sides spent Christmas awaiting 'the day appointed between them respecting the time of battle'. It should, however, be noted that the Abbot was a staunch Yorkist with a vehement hatred for the Lancastrians, especially after the second battle of St Albans in February 1461, when the victorious Lancastrians had plundered not only the town, but the abbey as well. Therefore, it is likely that in writing his account he painted as black a picture of the Lancastrians as possible – and demonstrating their dishonour by including the fact that they broke the truce in order to gain the advantage at the battle at Wakefield.
21. Waurin, p. 326.

Chapter Three

1. For an understanding of the campaign and battle of Bosworth, I suggest that the following should be consulted: M. Bennett, *The Battle of Bosworth* (Sutton Publishing, 1985), and my own *Military Campaigns of the Wars of the Roses* (Sutton Publishing, 1995), pp. 141–65.
2. Butler, pp. 26–7.
3. Ibid., p. 29

Chapter Four

1. See Appendix II for further chronicled descriptions, and also the works of Markham, Freeman and Leadman, who were able, to varying degrees, to view the undeveloped battlefield.
2. For the benefit of those unfamiliar with Burne's work, an explanation. Burne wrote many works on battles and battlefields (but sadly not Wakefield) and would weigh up the pros and cons of each suggested battlefield and apply IMP to determine its feasibility. For Burne's own explanation, see *The Battlefields of England*, pp. xiii–xiv.
3. Brooke, pp. 61–3.
4. See also the notes in Appendix I regarding the wooded areas in the Sandal area. These wooded areas were to play a significant role in the battle to come.

Chapter Five

1. There are a number of sources which give an account of the history of Sandal Castle during the English Civil War. Butler in *Sandal Castle Wakefield* (Wakefield Historical Society), pp. 86–103, covers the period well. A shortened version by Patrick Ray is given in Vol. 44 of *The English Civil War – Notes and Queries*, pp. 3–7. It is also mentioned in Dave Cooke's *The Forgotten Battle – Adwalton Moor* (Battlefield Press, 1996).
2. Stow, p. 683.
3. Davies, p. 106.
4. See Brooke's notes on Wiltshire's presence on the battlefield in Appendix II.
5. The reference to 'Sir' Andrew Trollope is incorrect, as he was not knighted until after the battle of St Albans the following February.
6. Markham, pp. 112–13.
7. Hall, p. 249.
8. Ibid., pp. 249–50.
9. Stow, p. 683.
10. Leadman, p. 354.
11. Vergil, p. 108.
12. Hall, p. 250
13. Stow, p. 684.
14. For further information regarding troop deployments during the battles of the Wars of the Roses, I suggest A.W. Boardman's *The Battle of Towton*. In Part Two of Goodman's *The Wars of the Roses* (pp. 117–226), there is an excellent account of 'Military Organisations and Society', including a chapter on 'Methods of Warfare'.
15. Vergil, p. 108.
16. Hall, p. 250.
17. Stow, p. 684.
18. Davies, p. 106.
19. Stansfield gives no source for this statement.
20. Stansfield, pp. 35–8.
21. Hutton says, 'The spot was about 400 yards from the Castle, close to the old road from Barnsley to Wakefield,' now called, from the sign of the public house, Cock and Bottle Lane. (The public house no longer exists, but its location can be found on the 1850s Ordnance Survey map.)
22. The location of this ring is today unknown.
23. Markham, pp. 113–14.
24. Tyas, pp. 59–60.
25. The well is clearly marked on both the 1850s and the 1914 Ordnance Survey map.
26. Brooke, pp. 64–5.
27. Again, Stansfield gives no source for these quotes.
28. Stansfield, pp. 40–1.
29. Hall, p. 250.
30. Stow, p. 684.
31. Vergil, p. 108.
32. Stansfield, p. 43.
33 Worc., p. 484.
34. Waurin, pp. 325–6.
35. Goodman, *The Wars of the Roses*, p. 42.
36. Stow, p6. 83.
37. Davies, pp. 106–7.
38. In the Middle Ages there were two main methods of recruiting troops. The first was 'livery and maintenance'. During the Hundred Years War, the English had a large standing army, established by contract with the nobles of the land, who paid for the troops and supplied captains to control and direct them. However, as the Hundred Years War came to an end, the need for a large army decreased, and by the middle of the fifteenth century, the official English army consisted only of the Calais garrison, whose task was to protect the sole remaining English possession in France at that time.

This meant that during the late 1450s and early 1460s there were to be found vast numbers of unemployed 'professional' men-at-arms, with little or no soldiering to do. Instead they found employment in the service of powerful English nobles, which meant that the likes of the Earl of Northumberland and the Earl of Warwick could enjoy the power and prestige of their own personal armies. Service to the lord was offered in return for the lord's protection in many matters, for example in legal issues. The lords in turn owed allegiance to the sovereign who could call on them and their private armies in times of need. With respect to the Wars of the Roses it was a matter of personal loyalty that swayed each lord between one side and the other – or in Wakefield's case, the King and the Protector. The principals would usually summon the lords and their troops by written communication. The following is an extract from a letter written by the Duke of Norfolk to the Pastons asking them to join with him to support Richard III against Henry Tudor at the time of the battle of Bosworth:

. . . and that ye bring with you such a company of tall men as ye may goodly make at my cost and charge and I pray you ordain them jackets of my livery, and I shall content you at your meeting with me.[46]

In the event, the Pastons chose to ignore the request!

The second way of recruiting men was by 'Commission of Array'. The King (or Protector) could issue a commission of array to any noble, which in effect meant that the recipient could recruit in the King's name and on his behalf, the men from the shires between the age of 16 and 60, in the defence of the realm. In practice, a central gathering point would be assigned and the levies required to attend at an appointed time. Messages had to be sent around the shires informing people of the muster, and time allowed for the gathering. This method of recruiting from the shires was of Anglo-Saxon origin, and the response was dependent on each shire's strength of allegiance to the King. Although, in some instances, failure to answer the summons could be punishable by death, it did nevertheless on occasion go unanswered.

A good example of an extant commission is the Bridport Muster Roll, which formed part of a commission of array in 1457. In this particular muster some 12,000 men were gathered from southern England for Henry VI. In trying to discover who was present at a battle during the Wars of the Roses, the probability of finding a single muster roll for each side is unlikely. As each side raised its army, a number of commissions would have been issued, and thus several sources (or muster rolls), would have to be compiled.

For further details regarding recruitment I suggest that the following works are consulted: M. Hicks, *Bastard Feudalism* (Longman, 1995), and C. Carpenter, *Locality and Polity* (Cambridge, 1992). Concise and comprehensive accounts of recruiting can be found in both A.W. Boardman's *The Battle of Towton* (Sutton Publishing, 1995), pp. 55–7, and Section Two of Goodman's *The Wars of the Roses*, particularly Chapter Six, 'Military Convention and Recruitment'.

39. *See* A.W. Boardman's *The Battle of Towton*, pp. 73–5.
40. Waurin, pp. 325–6.
41. Hall, p. 250.
42. Worc., pp. 484–5.
43. Ibid.
44. Davies, pp. 106–7.
45. Waurin, p. 326.
46. Paston Letters, vol. 6, p. 85.

Chapter Six

1. Brooke, p. 59.
2. Hall, pp. 250–1.
3. Worc., p. 485.
4. Stow, p. 684.
5. This is mentioned by Worcester (p. 485) and later by Goodman (p. 43) and Gillingham (p. 120).

6. For this, and other infamous 'deeds', he is also credited with the name 'Black-Faced' and 'Black-Hearted Clifford'.
7. Leland, vol. I, p. 43.
8. J.W. Walker, 'St Mary's Chapel on Wakefield Bridge' , *Yorkshire Archaeological Journal*, vol. 11, p. 154.
9. A. W. Boardman, *The Battle of Towton*, p. 30.
10. Stansfield says at a point where Leigh Street join Kirkgate, whereas Leadman says that it was where Park Street joins Kirkgate. By contrast Tyas (p. 60) states that Rutland was killed upon the 'Fallings', before he actually got to the bridge or Kirkgate (Wakefield).
11. The site was formerly pointed out as close to an ancient six-gabled house, with three gables in front and three behind. Its location is, however, near the bottom of Kirkgate just where Park Street joins it, a little above where the railway station stands today. As to the building itself, it simply collapsed in 1941, while the owner was engaged in a dispute with Wakefield Council over the price the council had offered to buy the property. After its collapse, the council promptly withdrew their offer and the owner was left to pay for the clearance of the site unaided.
12. Barrett, pp. 136–7.
13. Worc., *Annales Rerum Anglicarum*, vol. II, ed. Stevenson (1884).
14. Markham, pp. 106–7.
15. Stanfield, pp. 43–4.
16. Worc., p. 485.
17. Ibid.
18. The reason why the commons 'loved him not', was because Salisbury was the official receiver of those parts, and as such, in the years before the battle, he had become distinctly unpopular with the local people in the course of carrying out his official duties.
19. Stow, p. 413.
20. Davies, p. 107.
21. Hall, p. 251.
22. On p. 223 of Johnson's work *Duke Richard Of York 1411–1460*, reference is made to Salisbury's widow making claim to the fact that it was one John Sharp, gentleman of Pontefract, who executed the earl and not the 'Bastard of Exeter'. There are also other versions: Wolffe, in *Henry VI*, p. 327, records that the Countess of Salisbury claimed that nine obscure men aided by retainers of Sir Ralph Percy were responsible. However, the Earl of Warwick, Salisbury's son and heir, believed it was Holland. Less than three months after Salisbury's death, Warwick, marching with the Yorkist army towards Towton, captured Holland at Coventry, and had him summarily executed in a similar manner.
23. Hall, p. 251.
24. Virgil, p. 108.
25. Stow, p. 684.
26. Hall, p. 251.
27. Stow, p. 684.
28. Worc, p. 485.
29. Vergil, p. 108.
30. *See* R.L. Storey *The End of the House of Lancaster*, p. 194, for a fuller account of who was responsible for Salisbury's death.

Chapter Seven

1. In Patrick Ray's account of the siege of Sandal Castle (vol. 44 of *The English Civil War – Notes and Queries*, pp. 3–7), reference is made to Parliamentarian troops destroying the cross.
2. Butler, pp. 104–7.
3. H.C. Haldane, 'Relics of the battle of Wakefield 1460', *Yorkshire Archaeological Journal*, vol. 22, p. 128.
4. K. Dockray/R. Knowles, *The Battle of Wakefield*, p. 27.
5. Freeman, p. 277.
6. Ibid., pp. 278–9.
7. However, it is more than likely, despite the absence of contemporary evidence to prove it, that

when Edward IV visited the site and instructed that a monument be erected to the memory of his father (for which contemporary evidence does exist), then at the same time he also re-endowed the chapel in memory of his brother who died near that spot.

8. *Pat. Rol.*, 16 Ed. III, p. I, m. 34.
9. J.W. Walker, 'St Mary's Chapel on Wakefield Bridge', *Yorkshire Archaeological Journal*, vol. 11, p. 144–8.
10. Ibid., pp. 159–65.
11. Leeds Sessions, 19 October, 1842.
12. Shown in the *Ecclesiologist*.
13. J.W. Walker, 'St Mary's Chapel on Wakefield Bridge', *Yorkshire Archaeological Journal*, vol. 11, pp. 154–8.
14. Ibid., pp. 158–9.
15. Brooke, p. 62.
16. See also vol. 44 of *English Civil War – Notes and Queries*, pp. 3–7, where reference is made to the forces of Parliament destroying the cross that was erected to commemorate the death of the Duke of York.

Chapter Eight

1. Brooke, p. 63.
2. An account of the widespread plundering by the Lancastrians during their march to St Albans can be found in C.L. Scofield's *The Life and Reign of Edward IV* (1923), vol. I, pp. 135–6. See also Gregory's Chronicle, p. 212, and the English Chronicle, p. 107.
3. *Croyland Abbey Chronicle*, p. 531.
4. For an understanding of the campaign and battle of St Albans (1461), I suggest that the following should be consulted: A.H. Burne, *Battlefields of England* (Methuen, 1950), pp. 83–95, and my own *Military Campaigns of the Wars of the Roses* (Sutton Publishing, 1995), pp. 46–54.
5. For further details regarding Edward IV's accession to the throne see (contemporary) Worcester, vol. II, p. 777. For a more modern view see Ross, *Edward IV*, pp. 32–5. For details of Edward's coronation on Sunday 28 June 1461, see C.L. Scofield, *The Life and Reign of Edward IV* (1923), vol. I, pp. 181–4, and Ross, pp. 41–2.
6. *The Great Chronicle of London*, pp. 194–5.
7. Goodman, *The Wars of the Roses'*, p. 42.
8. Boardman, *The Battle of Towton*, p. 46.
9. Without doubt, the most complete account of the battle of Towton is A.W. Boardman's *The Battle of Towton* (Sutton Publishing, 1994).
10. The subject of York's reburial at Fotheringhay is covered in detail in 'The Reburial of Richard Duke of York 21–30 July 1476', in *The Ricardian*, 1994, vol. X, no. 127, pp. 122–55.
11. St Richard's Friary used to stand on a spot opposite what is now the general hospital, close to the A645 Pontefract–Knottingley road. However, it should be noted that the location of the Duke of York's interim resting place is hotly disputed, and a number of alternative sites have been suggested. For example, in Boothroyd's, *The History of the Ancient Borough of Pontefract*, (1807), p. 131, it is stated that the duke was laid to rest in the priory of St John. This location is also given in Fox's *The History of Pontefract* (1827), p. 151, and Dr Walker's *Wakefield: its History and People*, p. 168. L. Padgett, however, in the *Chronicles of Old Pontefract* (1905), p. 123, supports the view that St Richard's was indeed the place where the Duke was laid to rest.
12. Leland, vol. I, fo. 6

Appendix I

1. PRO, SC11/981, Rent Roll of the Manor of Wakefield.
2. K. Dockray/R. Knowles, *The Battle of Wakefield*, pp. 22–3.
3. The map is reproduced in a modern book titled *The Counties of Britain, A Tudor Atlas by John Speed*. 1988.

Appendix II

1. For further reading regarding the chroniclers, I suggest that the following are consulted: K.B. McFarlane's *England in the Fifteenth Century* (Hambelton, 1981); C.L. Kingsford's *English Historical Literature in the 15th Century* (1913); and Antonia Gransden's *Historical Writings in England* (London, 1982).

Appendix III

1. Sir William Parr(e) (ancestor of Queen Catherine Parr, Henry VIII's sixth wife), is said by some to have escaped the battlefield and was neither captured nor executed. Indeed Sir William Parr commanded the Earl of Warwick's cavalry at the battle of Edgecote on 26 July 1469 against Edward IV's army under the field command of the Earls of Devon and Pembroke. However, two years later in 1471 it appears that he had reverted to the Yorkist cause and supported Edward IV at the battle of Barnet (ironically against Warwick) and Tewkesbury (against the Lancastrians). For these later acts, he was well rewarded and remained highly placed within the Yorkist Household afterwards.
2. According to the chronicler Fabyan (p. 210), Harrow and Hanson were executed at Pontefract along with the Earl of Salisbury.
3. See note 2.
4. Barrett, p. 139.
5. Brooke wrote: 'James Boteler or Butler, the son and heir of James, 4th Earl of Ormond, was created Earl of Wiltshire in the 27th [year of the reign of] Henry VI. In the 30th year of Henry VI, by the death of his father, he also became Earl of Ormond. He was a staunch Lancastrian, and fought for that party at the first battle of St Albans in 1455; also the battle of Wakefield, and again at Mortimer's Cross. He appears also to have been at the battle of Towton. After that battle he was captured by the Yorkists, and was beheaded upon the 1st of May, 1461, at Newcastle. It is very remarkable, that although historians state that he fought on the Lancastrian side at the battle of Wakefield, and although he was attainted by the act 1st Edward IV [1461], his name is not amongst those of the nobleman and others, who were attainted for taking part in the battle of Wakefield . . . the fact of the Earl of Wiltshire having fought at the battle of Mortimer's Cross, is mentioned not only by old historians, but also in Rot. Parl. 1st Edward IV. Vol. V. p462; but that is not alleged in the act as the reason for his attainder. It does not seem easy to understand how he could be engaged at the battle of Wakefield, and be so soon afterwards at the head of the forces fighting at Mortimer's Cross.'
6. Markham, pp. 107–9.
7. In addition to the ones listed above, there are a number of other references to nobles present at the battle of Wakefield. J.C. Wedgwood's *History of Parliament*, Biographies, 1439–1509 (HMSO, 1936), makes reference to the following as being present:
    Sir Gervase Clifton (1416–91); Thomas Colt (1425–71) (of whom it is written that one Roger Thorpe, his Lancastrian rival, 'sought out Colt and attacked and sore hurt him' – Scofield, *Edward IV*, p. 35); Everard Digby (1410–61); William Feilding (1415–71); Sir Thomas Fynderne (1420–64); Sir William Grimsby (1420–82); Sir James Strangeways (1415–80) (according to a Clement Paston letter, was present at the battle); Sir Richard Tunstall (1427–92); Sir Robert Whittingham (1420–71).
    Yet another reference to other nobles present at the battle can be found in vol. 16 of the *Hobilar*, where Robert Hildyard Esq. of Winestead is mentioned as being present. Thomas Babthorpe, who was related to Hildyard, as was Sir John Hotham of Hotham (Yorkshire) – who was married to Hildyard's daughter, Isabel – were both also said to be present.
8. Barrett, p. 138.
9. Brooke, p. 56.

Appendix V

1. Waurin, p. 327.

Index